80p

A

OLIVER and MICHE… and macrobiotic medicine in London, the USA and Switzerland. Since 1983 they have lived and worked in Cornwall, where they run a range of courses in natural healthcare and cookery.

They have written widely on the subject of natural and healthy foods, including several books on macrobiotic cookery. They have two children, who have been brought up on a yin-yang diet.

OPTIMA

# YIN-YANG COOKBOOK

OLIVER AND MICHELE COWMEADOW

ILLUSTRATED BY MICHELE COWMEADOW

An OPTIMA book



First published in 1988 by
Macdonald Optima, a division of
Macdonald & Co. (Publishers) Ltd

A member of Maxwell Pergamon Publishing Corporation plc



British Library Cataloguing in Publication Daeta

Cowmeadow, Oliver
Yin Yang cookbook.
1. Food recipes
I. Title
641.5

ISBN 0-356-15196-4

Macdonald & Co. (Publishers) Ltd
3rd Floor
Greater London House
Hampstead Road
London NW1 7QX

Typeset by Leaper & Gard Ltd, Bristol, England
Printed and bound in Great Britain by
The Guernsey Press Co. Ltd
Guernsey
Channel Islands

# CONTENTS

# 1. THE YIN AND YANG OF FOOD

## THE SYMMETRY OF NATURE

If you think of any way we measure and describe the world, we always use pairs of characteristics. We have hot and cold, light and dark, up and down, hard and soft, male and female, happy and unhappy, wealth and poverty. In other words this world is relative — we describe anything by comparing it with something else. 'Hot' only has meaning in relation to 'cold', and 'happiness' when compared to 'unhappiness'. Everywhere in nature and in our lives we can see examples of this grand symmetry.

Yin and yang are used to describe all these pairs of opposite qualities. For example, hot, light and male are yang, and cold, dark and female are yin. To understand why and how yin and yang are used it helps to look at the ancient Oriental and worldwide view of nature. In all great cultures, philosophies and religions, there has been a concept of an infinite and absolute state, called Infinite Oneness, God, Brahman, or the large Self. In this state there is no division into time and space, or any other pair of qualities. It is undivided, infinite and eternal. This state is beyond our normal perception. Awareness of this state has been the goal of religions and other teachings for thousands of years.

The Infinite Oneness creates the relative world that we are all familiar with through a number of stages. First it divides into two opposite tendencies or yin and yang. From these is formed the most immaterial and diffuse part of our relative world — the level of energy and vibration (including light, heat, and other electromagnetic waves). This energy then becomes more concentrated to form sub-atomic particles, which combine to form atoms. Atoms of oxygen, carbon, hydrogen and other elements make up our physical environment — the air, sea and land.

From the physical environment, life arises. Plants absorb light from the sun and take up air, water and minerals from the soil and convert these into organic plant material. Animals eat plants, so from the plant world the animal world is created. As the highest evolved animal, the human species comes at the end of this path of creation. We take in all the preceding stages — Infinite Oneness, yin and yang, sunlight and other energy vibrations, air, water, plants and animals. In a large sense these are all our 'food'.

If any great teaching is examined, such as the Old Testament (especially the book of Genesis). The Taoist Te Ching, Buddhist teachings, and others, you will find that they all have this same basic conception of our creation. In Taoism this scheme is depicted in the well-known symbol shown below. The outer circle representing Infinite Oneness, which encircles the light and dark halves representing yang and yin.

We can now understand better why yin and yang are so useful in understanding our food, health and lives. Yin and yang have created everything in the relative world. Also, energy forms and nourishes the physical and living environment, including our food, life and health. In Japan this energy is called *Ki*, in China *Chi*, in India *Prana*, and in Western culture *Life Energy* or *Life Force*. Looking at our food, health and lives in terms of yin and yang and energy gives a profound understanding of the forces that have created nature, our food, and our daily experiences of life.

Yin is defined as energy or movement that is expanding and yang is the name given to energy or movement that is contracting. These two simple tendencies of expansion and contraction combine and interact to create all the pairs of opposite qualities that make up our relative world. For example, plants have a more expanded form, with many leaves and numerous roots in the soil, while the body of an animal is compact with their 'leaves' internally in the lungs and their 'roots' concentrated along the length of the intestines. Plants are therefore defined as yin and animals as yang.

Yin and yang produce the expansion and contraction of the heart and lungs and the rhythmic movements of the intestines. We may feel more expansive or extrovert or more inward-looking and introvert. Anger is a sudden outburst or explosion and receptivity is the ability to take in or receive. In this way any quality can be seen to be produced by either yin or yang.

## FOOD AS ENERGY

The current scientific way of looking at foods is in terms of *quantity* — the amount of nutrients like vitamins, minerals and protein that a food contains. With yin and yang we are looking at the energetic *quality* of foods. This quite different view greatly extends our understanding of the effect of foods on our health. Let us take the example of a carrot. We could analyse it to find the amount of carbohydrate, water or vitamin A it contains. However if we put the correct amounts of all these nutrients together, we would not make a carrot. Some essential component would be missing — the life energy of the carrot. This life energy actually created the carrot in the first place, by organizing the arrangement of atoms and nutrients into a definite 'carrot' form.

Alternatively, consider what would happen if all your food (breakfast, lunch, tea, supper, everything!) were put into a liquidizer and turned into a liquid mush. All the nutrients would still be there, but how long do you think you could live on this? Besides the boredom of eating this bland mush, one's vitality and health would soon begin to decline. The variety of different types of life energy from the various foods would have been largely destroyed by the liquidizing, and our health depends on these as much as on the nutrients in foods.

## WHICH FOODS ARE YIN AND WHICH ARE YANG?

How do we decide which foods are yin and which are yang? There are two ways of discovering the answer to this question. The first is through experience. When a more yang food is put into the mouth, it is possible to feel the changes it creates. For example one may feel a contraction or tightening in organs like the stomach, intestines or bladder, increased tension, or a warming of the body. Eating a more yin food produces opposite changes. These changes become stronger as the food is digested and taken into the blood and body over the next few hours and days. Generally this sense is dulled by the long-term eating of extreme yin and yang foods, but you may still feel the effects of some foods on your body and moods. This sense is greatly increased when one follows the yin-yang balanced diet described in this book, simply by observing how one feels after eating certain foods and meals.

Because it takes time to develop this level of perception to foods, it helps to begin with a second more intellectual way of understanding which foods are yin and which are yang. This also gives a structure to help us order our more intuitive perceptions of the effects of foods. From the definition and examples of yin and yang given above, we can draw up some useful points of comparison between the yin and yang characteristics of foods — see chart on page 11. A few examples will make the use of these characteristics clearer. As we have already said, the compact nature of animals means that they are more yang than the expanded form of plants. So animal foods like meat, poultry and eggs are more yang than plant foods like cereal grains, vegetables and fruits. Among plant foods, whole grains like rice and barley are small, hard and compact when compared with vegetables and fruits, and so are more yang than fruit and vegetables. Fruits also have a higher proportion of potassium to sodium than vegetables and are more cooling, so they are more yin. Whole grains and beans are similar in size and hardness, but the slightly larger size and higher protein and fat content of beans indicate that they are more yin than whole grains.

There can be a lot of variation in yin and yang quality even within one food group. For instance fruits growing in hotter or tropical climates, like oranges or bananas, are far more yin than apples or strawberries. This is shown by their much higher potassium content. The same is true of vegetables that have originated from the tropics, including tomatoes, potatoes and aubergines, even though they may now be grown in colder climates.

The way foods are prepared or processed from basic animal or plant matter can affect their yin and yang characteristics. Extracts of plants are generally yin. Sugar, for example, mainly comes from sugar cane, a tropical plant, indicating a more yin nature. Then in the process of extracting a small quantity of sugar from a large amount of sugar cane, the most yin part of the sugar cane is isolated. This makes sugar an extremely yin food. The same is true of other plant extracts like coffee, tea, cocoa, carob and spices. Fermentation of any food also makes it more yin, especially if alcohol is produced. So fermenting grains to make beer or spirits and fermenting fruits to make wine will also produce a more yin 'food'. Dairy foods are another example. They can vary a great deal in their yin and yang nature, depending on how they have been prepared. The watery nature

| | YANG | YIN |
|---|---|---|
| All Foods | animal foods<br>high in sodium<br>drier<br>bitter-salty-sweet[1]<br>smaller size<br>saturated fat<br>saltier[2]<br>warming the body<br>oil-soluble vitamins<br>e.g. $B_1$, $B_2$, $B_{12}$, C | plant foods<br>high in potassium<br>wetter, moister<br>sweet-sour-spicey<br>larger size<br>unsaturated fat<br>less salty<br>cooling the body[3]<br>water-soluble vitamins<br>e.g. A, D, E, K |
| Animal Foods | more active animals<br>warm blooded animals<br>black-red-brown<br>minerals-protein | less active animals<br>cold blooded animals<br>white-transparent<br>protein-fat |
| Plant Foods | temperate climate plants<br>harvested in autumn and winter<br>slow growth rate<br>less aromatic<br>smaller, harder<br>minerals-carbohydrates | tropical plants<br>harvested in spring and summer<br>fast growth rate<br>more aromatic<br>larger, softer<br>protein-fats-oil |

**Qualities used for Establishing the Yin or Yang Nature of Foods**

1. The sweet taste is the natural sweetness of onions, parsnips, fruits etc and not the artificial sweetness of sugar and foods with added sugar.
2. Salt is extremely yang; it is 50 per cent sodium without any potassium.
3. Extremely yin foods such as sugar and spices may be felt to warm the surface of the body at first, but are actually cooling deep inside the body in the long term.

of milk and its high fat content indicate that it is more yin in nature — approximately the same as fruit. Milk can then be made even lighter and more fatty or yin by turning it into cream, or harder, saltier and more compacted or yang by using it to make butter and cheese.

Processed and pre-packaged foods are often composed of several foods, which have quite different qualities. Crisps, for example, contain a tropical vegetable, oil and usually chemical additives — all fairly yin. However, they are usually very salty — a yang quality. So crisps contain both extreme yin and yang qualities.

By thinking of the yin and yang characteristics of foods in the way that has just been described, all foods can be arranged on a scale from yang to yin, as shown in the chart on page 13.

## UNDERSTANDING OUR FOOD PREFERENCES

A universal law of nature and life is that all changes and actions tend to move towards balance. As a part of nature we do not escape this universal law. So if we eat a yang food, we are attracted to eating some yin food. If we eat a more yin type of food, we feel that we should like to eat something yang. This act of making balance is usually quite unconscious, even though it is a major factor in determining what we choose to eat. For example, if you eat something salty, you then want a drink. You may drink a pint of beer, then eat some salty crisps or nuts, then more beer, and so on. Salty snacks are provided in pubs for a very good reason!

A look at the major constituents of anyone's diet will reveal how they make up a balance between yin and yang foods. Anyone who eats a lot of meat always balances this with sugar, biscuits, cakes and other sweet foods. Vegetarians may not be eating meat or poultry, but often consume eggs, cheese and especially wholemeal bread, which is generally pretty salty and with its dry baked quality is a particularly yang form of grain. They may then balance this with sugar, honey, tropical fruits and vegetables. If you examine your own eating patterns, you can discover how you are balancing the yin and yang in your diet.

An unconscious need to balance yin and yang also accounts for many traditional ways of combining foods. In Britain, lamb is accompanied by mint sauce, beef with horseradish, pork with apple sauce and chicken is stuffed with herbs. With eggs and sausages a tomato or spicy sauce is favoured and beefburgers generally come with a fruity pickle or relish. Pickles also go well with cheese and lemon juice with fish. Think of your favourite combinations and you will discover how you are already balancing yin and yang.

It is sad that this very simple principle of balance between yin and yang foods is not more widely understood. Many a valiant effort to give up or reduce sugar, cakes or coffee has ended in failure for the simple reason that the consumption of salt, eggs, meat or cheese has not also been reduced. Then the body of course craves yin and sooner or later it generally gets it!

## Foods Arranged on a Scale from Yang to Yin

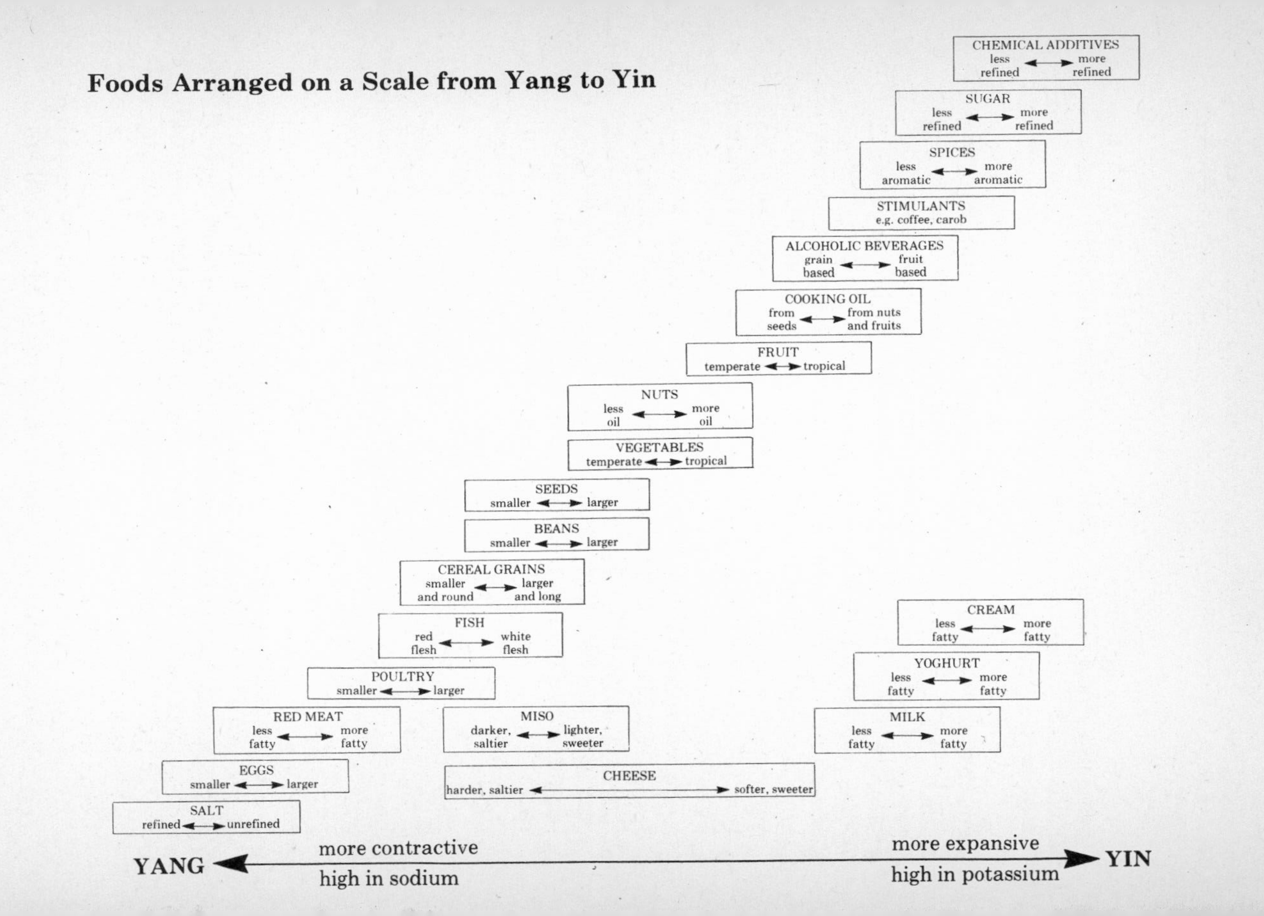

Attempts to reduce addiction to alcohol or drugs are made much easier by reducing or cutting the most yang foods out of the diet.

## THE ACID-ALKALINE BALANCE

The proportion of acid to alkaline substances in the blood and body fluids is another example of a balance between opposites that must be maintained for health. Our blood should be slightly alkaline (around a pH of 7.4) for us to enjoy good health. The main factor determining the acid-alkaline balance of the body is the food we eat.

You may think that acid and alkaline forming foods might correlate with yin and yang foods. Unfortunately it is not so simple. Whether foods create an acid or alkaline condition depends on their mineral content. Foods high in phosphorous, sulphur or chlorine form acids, and foods containing much sodium, potassium, calcium or magnesium have an alkalizing effect. A summary of acid- and alkaline-forming foods is given in the chart below.

As with balancing yin and yang foods, we unconsciously create a crude balance between acid- and alkaline-forming foods by choosing foods from both categories. Depending on the foods we choose, we may keep close to the ideal — slightly alkaline, or we may fluctuate widely between a more acid and alkaline

| **ACID FORMING** | **ALKALINE FORMING** |
|---|---|
| most chemicals | coffee and tea |
| medicinal and halucinogenic drugs | fruit |
| sugar, honey and sweets | vegetables |
| soft drinks | sea vegetables |
| most alcoholic drinks | seeds |
| beans | shoyu |
| nuts | miso |
| cereal grains | umeboshi |
| fish | salt |
| poultry | |
| meat | |
| eggs | |

**Acid- and Alkaline-Forming Foods**

condition. To keep a steady balance it is helpful to primarily eat foods from the centre of the yin-yang scale, which in general are only mildly acid- and alkaline-forming. The foods at the two ends of the yin-yang scale, such a meat, sugar and drugs have stronger acid- and alkaline-forming effects.

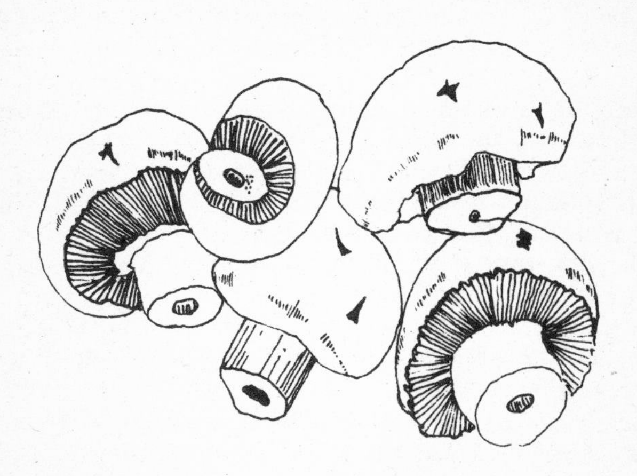

## THE WAY TO BETTER HEALTH

The most fundamental way of achieving balance in health and life is through the food we eat. By eating foods from the centre of the yin-yang scale (see page 13) and avoiding extreme yin and yang foods our energy will become more balanced.

Food is first absorbed into the blood, so it is here that balance first occurs. Within days and weeks of eating a balanced yin-yang diet, you will feel brighter, more energetic and sleep better. Minor problems, like headaches, fatigue and small infections will disappear. The blood nourishes all the cells and organs of the body, so over weeks and months various bodily functions will improve. Muscle tension and aches and pains may recede. You may feel calmer and less stressed. Eventually, over months and years, the form and structure of the body can change, mostly noticeably in loss of fat deposits. You will feel fitter, more alert and have more stamina. All this will make everyday problems easier to cope with, leading to a more enjoyable and fulfilling life.

# 2.
# WHAT TO EAT

Now we can look in detail at the foods that make up a healthy balanced diet. A diet centred around grains, beans and vegetables strikes some people as a recipe for boredom, but I think you will agree after reading this chapter that the variety is endless. Quite probably you will find a greater variety of ingredients, recipes, and tastes than you are eating at the moment.

The ideal proportion of each food group in your daily diet by volume on your plate is given after each food group. Where some varieties are better balanced or more healthy and can be eaten as often as you like, they are listed as *For regular use.* Varieties that are fine to eat but not so often are listed as *For frequent use.* Foods which have a too extreme yin or yang nature to be part of a healthy balanced diet are listed under *To avoid.*

We have assumed that readers are living in a temperate climate, such as northern Europe, North America or Canada. If you are living in a hotter climate such as Australia or northern New Zealand, slightly different foods will be appropriate. For example, long grain rice could be used more frequently and a moderate amount of tropical fruits could be eaten. Although some of the varieties may differ, the ideal proportions of the different food groups remain the same.

## PRINCIPAL FOODS

Principal foods are those that form an essential part of a well-balanced diet. They make up 80 to 90 per cent of an ideal diet.

### Whole Cereal Grains (35-50 per cent)

*For regular use*
buckwheat, corn on the cob, millet, pot and pearl barley, whole oats (oat groats), short and medium grain brown rice, rye, whole wheat

*For frequent use*
buckwheat noodles (soba), barley flakes, bulghur, corn grits and

cornmeal, couscous, long grain brown rice, ramen noodles (wholewheat, rice or buckwheat), rice cakes, rice flakes, rolled oats, rye flakes, seitan and fu (made from wheat gluten), somen (sifted wholewheat noodles), sweet brown rice and pounded sweet rice (mochi), udon (wholewheat noodles), wholemeal bread and pita bread, wholewheat crackers, wholewheat noodles and pasta

*To avoid*
white bread, white flour and all white or refined flour products

Whole grains are close to the centre of the yin-yang scale of foods and form the largest food group. They can form part of every meal. They should mainly be eaten in their whole form, that is as complete grains. This way they contain the maximum amount of nutrients and vitality and are also most easily digested. Flour products made from whole grains can be eaten in smaller amounts (noodles, bread etc). Too many of these flour products can cause difficulties with digestion and create mucus in the lungs, sinuses, nose and other parts of the body.

The main ways of cooking whole grains are boiling and pressure cooking. Short and medium grain brown rice is much more delicious pressure cooked. Rice is particularly versatile and combines well with many other foods. Rice cooked with barley, wheat, millet, aduki beans or chestnuts is delicious and provides a welcome change to just plain rice. It can also be mixed with roasted seeds or nuts or with vegetables to make a rice salad. Long grain rice, millet and buckwheat are better boiled and also combine well with vegetables.

Sweet rice is a delicious form of rice that is more glutinous and higher in protein and is rich and sweet tasting. In Japan it is traditionally pounded into a firm sticky dough called *mochi*, which can be used in savoury and sweet dishes. Mochi can also be bought in dried form from some shops. If you have any problems obtaining sweet rice or dried mochi, please refer to the list of suppliers in the Appendix on page 160.

## Vegetables (25-35 per cent)

*For regular use*
green vegetables — bok choy, broccoli, brussel sprouts, cabbage, Chinese cabbage, chives, collard greens, kale, leeks, lettuce, mustard greens, parsley, spring greens, spring onions and watercress
root vegetables — burdock, carrots, lotus root, mooli (daikon or long white radish), dried daikon, parsnips, orange and green pumpkins, radishes, rutabagas, salsify, swedes and turnips

*For frequent use*
alfalfa and bean sprouts, beets, broad breans, celery, courgettes, cucumbers, endive, french beans, marrow, mushrooms, mustard cress, peas, red cabbage, runner beans, shitake (Japanese dried mushrooms), Swiss chard

*To avoid*
artichokes, aubergine (egg plant), green peppers, potatoes, red peppers, spinach, sweet potatoes, tomatoes, yams

Vegetables offer a very wide range of colours, tastes and textures. They can be cut in many different sizes and shapes to add to their attractivenes. They can be cooked by boiling, steaming, sautéeing or frying and baking. They can also be eaten raw or lightly blanched, as pickles and in soups. In summer more salads and lightly cooked vegetables help us feel cooler and in winter more long-cooked dishes help us keep warm. In general the proportion of raw vegetables can vary between 5 and 25 per cent.

**Beans and Bean Products (5-10 per cent)**
*For regular use*
aduki beans, chick peas, green or brown lentils, natto, tempeh, tofu

*For frequent use*
blackeye beans, black soya beans, black turtle beans, great northern beans, haricot beans, lima beans, mung beans, navy beans, pinto beans, red lentils, split peas, soya milk

Beans and bean products are a rich source of protein. Many contain as much as meat. This is not 'complete protein', that is to say containing all the amino acids necessary for health, but when beans and grains are used together the grain protein provides the amino acids lacking in the beans. To supply us with our protein needs, several tablespoons of beans per day is quite enough for most people.

Beans have the reputation of causing flatulence in some people and so are often avoided. However this problem can generally be overcome with a little knowledge on how to cook them properly. Their high protein content does make them a little difficult to digest, but this can be overcome in the following ways:

- Add minerals by cooking the beans with a piece of sea vegetable, such as kelp or kombu, and seasoning with sea salt or shoyu soy sauce towards the end of cooking

- Cook the beans until soft all the way through. There should not be a powdery white centre left but an even colour all through the beans. For beans which take a long time to cook, such as chick peas, it is helpful to soak them for 8 hours or overnight to speed up the cooking time. They can also be pressure cooked.
- Don't eat too many at one time. One or two heaped tablespoons is plenty at one meal.

Before using beans, spread them out on a large plate or shallow baking tray and pick out any stones or other impurities. Then wash them in a sieve under a tap. There are many ways of preparing beans. They can be cooked on their own, with a grain like short or medium grain rice, combined with vegetables and in soups.

Several excellent products made from soya beans are becoming increasingly popular. *Tofu* is soya bean curd. It resembles a mild cheese, and is quick to cook in vegetable dishes, soups and in making salad dressings. Usually the tofu sold in shops comes as firm cakes, which can be used in both savoury and sweet dishes. Beware of soft or 'silken' tofu, which has very little taste and is too soft to use in most recipes. *Tempeh* (pronounced tem-pay) consists of firm cakes of soya beans bound by a white mold, and similarly can be used in many different recipes. *Soya milk* is commonly used as a replacement for cow's milk. However care should be taken not to use too much of it, as it is a lot more yin than the beans it is made from. Overuse can therefore be weakening to the intestines and body as a whole. This is especially true for small children.

## Sea Vegetables (3-4 per cent)

*For regular use*
agar-agar, arame, dulse, Irish moss (carrageen), hiziki, kelp, kombu, laver, mekabu, nori, wakame

Sea vegetables are incredibly rich in minerals, and a small quantity eaten regularly offers an invaluable source of essential minerals and trace elements. Dulse, for example, has 200 times more iron than beet greens, the richest land vegetable, and hizike has 14 times more calcium than cow's milk. Nori contains Vitamin $B_{12}$, which is generally absent in plant foods. With the present decline in the health of soils and the mineral content of foods grown on them, sea vegetables are perhaps a more important food now than they have ever been.

It has recently been discovered that regular consumption of sea vegetables has another great advantage for us in the modern age. Some of them contain alginic acid, a substance that transforms certain toxic or radioactive elements in the intestines into harmless salts that are easily eliminated from the body in the faeces. With our environment and food becoming increasingly contaminated with these very dangerous substances, regular use of sea vegetables could offer us some protection againt their harmful effects.

Sea vegetables are bought dried in packets. They often have a layer of salt encrusted on them, which can be removed with a quick rinse under water. The wide fronds of kelp and kombu can alternatively be wiped with a damp cloth.

Different varieties of sea vegetables have quite different tastes, textures and shapes and are best used in different ways. Dulse and wakame are thin fronds and are ideal in soups and salads. Kelp and kombu are rather thicker and need longer cooking, such as with beans or in a casserole or stew. Nori comes in thin sheets making it suitable for wrapping around other foods to create some very attractive dishes, such as traditional Japanese *sushi.* Arame and hiziki have their own unique flavour and texture and can be prepared as a vegetable dish. Agar-agar is used as a setting agent for making aspics and jellies (you have almost certainly eaten much of it already in foods like ice cream and many dressings).

### Fermented Foods (5 per cent)

*For regular use*
barley (mugi) miso, shoyu soy sauce, tamari, sauerkraut and other pickled vegetables made without sugar or artificial ingredients, tempeh, umeboshi (pickled green plums)

*For frequent use*
rice (genmai) miso, hatcho (pure soya bean) miso, white miso, traditionally brewed beer

*To avoid*
chemically produced pickles

Fermented foods have several unique properties. They contain micro-organisms and enzymes that are very beneficial for the digestive process, especially if the natural intestinal flora has been depleted by eating a lot of animal and processed foods or by taking antibiotics. The fermentation process also creates vitamins, including vitamin $B_{12}$. This particular vitamin is found only in animal foods, fermented foods and a few sea vegetables, so in vegetarian or near-vegetarian diets fermented foods play an important role in supplying this vitamin. Besides these advantages, fermented foods are also delicious and add a lot of variety to one's diet.

The traditional Far Eastern fermented foods made from soya beans are becoming increasingly popular in the West. *Miso*, a dark brown savoury paste, is ideal for seasoning soups, gravies and dressings. *Tamari* and *shoyu* soy sauce are great seasonings to use instead of salt, adding a rich flavour to vegetable and bean dishes. Be sure to get genuine shoyu soy sauce rather than many of the cheaper brands of soy sauce which are often no more than a cocktail of chemical additives and sugar.

The sour taste of sauerkraut and other pickled vegetables is a great stimulant to the appetite. It also improves digestion. Most commercial pickles contain acetic acid, sugar and many other artificial ingredients, but a few brands are made in the traditional way with just salt to promote the lactic fermentation of the vegetables. Pickles are also very easy to make at home.

## SECONDARY FOODS

Secondary foods are those which are eaten in smaller amounts or less often in a balanced and healthy diet. They are not as essential for health as the Principal Foods and different people may choose to eat more or less of them. In total they make up about 10 per cent of a healthy diet, though at first you may want to include more of them in your daily fare.

## Fish and Seafood

*For regular use*
white meat fish — including bass, carp, cod, dab, flounder, haddock, halibut, herring, plaice, scrod, sole, sprats, trout, turbot, whitefish, and whiting

*For frequent use*
eel, shark, blue skinned or red meat fish — including mackerel, salmon, sardines, tuna, crab, lobster, mussels, oysters, prawns and shrimps

Fish and seafood are the most suitable forms of animal food, as they are the least yang animal food. They also contain less saturated fats than meat, poultry and dairy foods. Fish has the added advantage of being harvested from the wild, so it is full of vitality and lacks the added hormones, antibiotics, colouring agents and preservatives that now so often come with meat and poultry. Among the many varieties of fish and seafood, the white meat fish are preferable for regular consumption due to their very low fat content. Shellfish, red meat and blue skinned fish are higher in cholesterol and fats and should be eaten less often.

Fish and seafood can be eaten two or three times a week as part of a balanced diet. It is a good idea to serve them with plenty of vegetables or a salad to create a better balance in the meal and to season them with a little vinegar, root ginger, lemon juice or other more yin seasoning.

## Fruit

*For regular use*
apples, apricots, blackberries, blueberries, cantaloupe melons, cherries, cranberries, currants (black and red), grapes, honeydew melons, peaches, pears, plums, prunes, raspberries, strawberries, water melons, any of the above in a dried form e.g. sultanas, raisins and dried apricots

*For frequent use*
lemon juice, sugar-free jams

*To avoid*
avocados, bananas, coconuts, dates, figs, grapefruits, guavas, kiwis, mangos, oranges, papayas, pineapples, pomegranates

Fruits are a sweet and delicious part of any diet. However it must be remembered that they come towards the yin end of the yin-yang food scale. It is therefore wise to use them only several times a week, or at the most a single helping daily. This may come as a surprise as they are often recommended in large quantities. When meat, eggs, cheese and other animal foods are eaten regularly, there is a great attraction for the cooling effect of fruits, but when less animal food is eaten consuming a lot of fruit can actually be quite weakening and devitalising. It is also best to avoid tropical fruits and choose varieties that grow in more temperate regions.

Fruit can be used in many dessert recipes such as crumbles, pies, jellies and puddings or can be simply stewed or baked. Uncooked fresh or dried fruits can also be eaten, though too much raw fruit can accentuate its cooling and weakening effects. It is obviously more appropriate to eat raw fruits in the heat of summer and to use more dried and cooked fruits in the winter.

## Seeds and Nuts

*For regular use*
pumpkin, sesame and sunflower seeds, almonds, chestnuts, hazelnuts, peanuts, pecans, walnuts

*To avoid*
carraway and poppy seeds, brazil, cashew, macadamia and pistachio nuts

Seeds and nuts provide us with plant oils in a natural state, as well as beautiful flavours and a good crunch. They have much more flavour if they are lighly roasted and this makes them much easier to digest as well. Seeds are most easily roasted in a dry frying pan (oil isn't needed as they contain so much oil already). They need to be frequently turned or stirred until a little darker in colour and giving off a beautiful aroma. Nuts are more easily roasted under a grill or in the oven. A few handfuls of seeds or nuts a week is plenty.

Various seed and nut butters like sesame spread, tahini, and peanut butter can also be used, but it is best to use them in small amounts due to their very oily nature. Peanut butter sandwiches should be an occasional treat rather than a daily lunch.

## Beverages

*For regular use*
grain coffee (yannoh or instant varieties), roasted barley tea, three-year twig tea (Bancha or Kukicha), well or spring water

*For frequent use*
apple juice, dandelion coffee, green tea, mu tea (a blend of non-stimulating herbs), non-aromatic herb teas e.g. camomile, traditionally brewed beers e.g. Guinness, sake, whisky, vegetables juices e.g. carrot juice

*To avoid*
aromatic herb teas e.g. mint and rose hip, black teas, coffee, decaffinated coffee, orange juice and juices of other tropical fruits and vegetables, sherry, soft drinks and artificially flavoured beverages, spirits, wine

It is amazing to realise that the most commonly used beverages are in fact quite unhealthy. Generally they are very yin, and are presumably chosen to make a balance with the large amount of yang animal foods in the modern diet. Many are stimulants, such as coffee, the usual brands of tea and the aromatic herb teas. Many contain a lot of sugar and alcohol is often drunk to excess. When eating a more balanced diet the need for such yin drinks diminishes and less extreme drinks become more attractive and satisfying. The *amount* of liquid consumed often falls as well, from five or ten or fifteen cups a day to three or four, with great benefits to health especially for the kidneys which have to process and get rid of all this liquid.

One of the best drinks to use regularly is three-year twig tea (also called Bancha or Kukicha). Most teas are made from the young leaves of the tea plant and contain much caffeine, whereas twig tea, made from the twigs, is very low in caffeine. It has a tea-like taste and is very refreshing, tasting fine without any milk or sugar.

A good brand of grain coffee (yannoh) is a must for any coffee addict. It can be simmered like twig tea or put in a percolator. A good strong brew makes a very satisfying alternative to coffee. There are also several brands of instant grain coffee that can be tried.

Fruit and vegetable juices are extracts of the most yin part of a food and so should be used in small amounts. Unsweetened apple juice is probably the best and can be used more often in the hot summer months.

Alcoholic beverages can be enjoyed from time to time in moderation. Alcohol being very yin, it is best to choose types that are made from the most yang plants — grains, like traditionally brewed beers, whisky and sake (rice wine).

## Snacks

*For frequent use*
crackers (sugar-and chemical-free), homemade popcorn, oat cakes (sugar-free), puffed wheat (sugar-free), rice cakes, roasted seeds, nuts and beans, vegetable and bean pâtés

*To avoid*
carob, chocolate, crisps, salted or dry roasted peanuts, sweets,

any commercial snacks containing sugar, honey, molasses or other form of sugar

Snacks form an important part of many people's diets. There is nothing wrong with snacking between meals if you are genuinely hungry, but the *quality* of the food eaten is important.

Roasted seeds and nuts make a delightfully crunchy snack and can be lightly seasoned with sea salt or shoyu soy sauce in the last minute or two of cooking for extra flavour. Homemade popcorn goes down well with children and rice cakes are often a favourite with adults and children alike. They are made of puffed rice grains and some say look rather like polystyrene, but they have satisfied many a yen for a crunchy snack. They can also be spread with a vegetable or bean pâté, humous, barley malt, sugar-free jam, and many other toppings. Crackers, water biscuits and oatcakes can also be used, but always check the ingredients list on the packet to make sure they do not contain sugar or chemical additives.

## Seasonings

*For regular use*
chives, horseradish, miso, mustard (sugar- and additive-free), parsley, rice vinegar, root ginger, sea salt, shoyu soy sauce, spring onions, tamari, umeboshi plums, umeboshi paste and vinegar

*For frequent use*
basil, bay leaf, garlic, lemon juice, oregano, tarragon, thyme, vanilla

*To avoid*
common salt, malt and wine vinegar, pepper (black or white), sauces containing sugar and chemical additives, spices

Seasonings provide variety in the tastes of dishes and are an important and necessary part of any diet. It interesting to see that practically all seasonings are either extremely yang (salt, miso, shoyu etc.) or extremely yin (spices, sugar, pepper, monosodium glutamate, chemical flavourings etc). Used in small amounts they add a strong yin or yang element to a dish, giving it a more interesting flavour and greater energy.

*Sea salt* — Many people have become aware that the modern diet contains far too much salt, contributing to problems like high blood pressure. This has led them to cut down on their use of salt in cooking or to following salt-free diets. Certainly for those who have over used salt in the past, a salt-free diet may be beneficial for a while, but in the long-term the body does require a small amount of this most yang 'food' for the proper functioning of the blood, nerves, muscles and other systems.

The best kind of salt to use is sea salt. Common salt is pure sodium chloride and often has dextrose (a form of sugar) and sodium-aluminate added to keep the salt white and easy to pour. Sea salt is simply produced by drying out sea water and contains many trace elements necessary for health such as copper, magnesium, calcium and nickel. This accounts for its milder flavour and better taste. Also, just use sea salt in cooking, not at the table. Cooking foods with a little salt adds to their flavour, whereas sprinkling it onto your food gives a sharp salty taste and creates excessive thirst. The condiments listed later are much better for this.

*Miso, shoyu soy sauce and tamari* — The benefits of eating these fermented soya bean products has already been discussed (see page 20). Besides their health benefits, they make delicious seasonings.

Miso is salty and hearty and most useful as the basis of a stock for soups. It also gives a delicious taste to sauces, gravies, spreads and dressings. There are several varieties to choose from. Barley (mugi) miso is the most balanced for everyday use, while the stronger hatcho miso (made without grains) is more suitable for occasional use in winter and in colder climates. Rice (genmai) miso is slightly lighter, especially good in summer and white miso is much sweeter making it good in sauces and dressings.

Shoyu soy sauce is a wonderful flavouring for soups, beans, vegetable dishes, spreads — in fact almost anything! It can be used in place of salt (it has a mildly salty taste) and has the advantage of adding more flavour to dishes. It is convenient to keep it in a small bottle with a perforated top so that it can be sprinkled over food as you cook.

Genuine tamari is the liquid drained off in the process of making miso and has a very strong flavour. The tamari that is widely sold today is made from soya beans and wheat in the same way as shoyu. Generally it has a slightly stronger taste than shoyu.

*Rice vinegar* — Commercially made vinegar is very acid and usually contains a good measure of chemical additives. Rice vinegar is produced traditionally by fermentation and is less acidic. It adds a nice sharp flavour to stir-fried vegetables, relishes, and to dressings for salads and vegetable dishes. If you cannot find rice vinegar the next best choice is cider vinegar.

*Root ginger, horseradish and mustard* — These are useful for providing a hot taste in dishes. For ginger, use the fresh roots rather than ginger powder or the dried sticks found in some shops. Most commonly the ginger is finely grated and cooked with the food. The juice can also be squeezed out of the grated ginger between the fingers onto the cooking. A little in soups, bean and vegetable dishes is delicious.

With horseradish and mustard, look for a more naturally prepared variety that doesn't have sugar and chemical additives in it. You may also come across *wasabi* or powdered Japanese horseradish, that is extremely hot!

*Umeboshi, umeboshi paste and umeboshi vinegar* — Umeboshi are a Japanese favourite — green plums pickled in sea salt with a unique sour and salty taste — that makes them a great seasoning with grains and in spreads and dressings. Umeboshi paste is the pulp of the pickled plums without the stones, which can be a more convenient form to use in making dressings. Umeboshi are highly valued for their strong alkalizing effect and are very effective at combatting an over-acid stomach and intestinal upsets. Umeboshi vinegar has the same sour-salty taste as the plums and can give a beautiful tanginess to sauces and dressings.

*Parsley, spring onions and chives* — These fresh vegetables can be chopped finely and used to add zest and colour to soups, bean and vegetable dishes.

*Kuzu and arrowroot* — These white powders are used to thicken sauces, gravies and certain desserts. Kuzu is made from the roots of the kuzu vine and is quite yang, whereas arrowroot is more yin. It is preferable to use kuzu in cooking but if you cannot find it arrowroot can be substituted.

If kuzu and arrowroot are added to hot liquids they form lumps, so they must be dissolved in a little cold water before adding to cooking. Both thickeners have no taste of their own and so can be used in savoury and sweet dishes.

*Herbs* — Herbs like bay leaf and thyme are more yin than the other seasonings described above and so should be used less often and in smaller amounts. In many people's cooking herbs have become the main flavour in many dishes, but this is really too much. Don't let them become a crutch for poor cooking. Traditionally herbs were used for their medicinal effects and were not usually used in any quantity on a daily basis. However using herbs sparingly in vegetable, bean or grain dishes can really enhance natural flavours.

## Condiments

*For regular use*
gomasio (sesame salt), mustard and horseradish (sugar-and chemical-free), roasted and powdered sea vegetables, sauerkraut and pickled vegetables, tekka, umeboshi

*To avoid*
mayonnaise, salt, sauces containing sugar, spices or chemical additives

Condiments are added to food at the table to add flavour and flair. One of the best to use regularly, especially if you are used to using salt on your food, is gomasio (sesame salt). This is made from roasted and ground sesame seeds mixed with a small amount of sea salt. It has a beautiful nutty aroma. It can be bought in many natural food shops, but do try making it yourself as the flavour is much better when freshly made. You can make enough to last for a few weeks at a time. Keep it in an air-tight jar.

A different salty taste can come from roasting a sea vegetable like wakame in a low oven until it is crisp, and then grinding it to a powder. Gomasio and roasted sea vegetable powder are especially good sprinkled on rice, noodles and other grain dishes.

## Sweeteners

*For regular use*
barley malt, rice syrup

*For frequent use*
concentrated apple juice, amasake, maple syrup

*To avoid*
white, brown or demerara sugar, molasses, honey, chemical sweeteners

Most people have become aware that sugar is one of the most harmful of modern 'foods', contributing to tooth decay, obesity, heart problems, diabetes, irregular blood sugar levels and the associated swings in mood between elation and depression. This includes not only white sugar but also any concentrated source of sugars such as honey, molasses and even an excess of fruit juices and concentrates. A further effect of sugar is to deplete the body of minerals. Because it has been stripped of the vitamins, minerals and fibre needed for its proper digestion and metabolism, these have to be taken from the body instead. The high consumption of sugar could be the main cause of mineral deficiencies today, rather than a lack of minerals in the rest of the diet. If you are worried about whether you are getting enough vitamins and minerals, think about reducing your sugar intake before reaching for the supplements.

However, we do actually need a fair amount of sweetness in our diet, but sugar is not the only source of sweetness. This taste (and energy) can come primarily from cooked onions, carrots, parsnips and other sweet vegetables on a daily basis. Then dried and fresh fruits can be used in smaller amounts. Also, two sweeteners made from grains — barley malt (malt extract) and rice syrup — can be used. They are richer in minerals and vitamins and although sweet are lower in sugar content. As well as sweetness, malt adds a delicious flavour to biscuits, cakes and puddings. Rice syrup has a more subtle flavour and can be used in more delicate tasting desserts. It's also great on pancakes and has a soothing effect if added to tea.

*Amasake* is a natural sweetener made from fermented brown rice or sweet rice. It can be bought ready-made or you can make it at home by mixing cooked rice with bought packets of rice coated in special micro-organisms called *koji.*

Concentrated apple juice can be used as a stronger sweetener in desserts. Maple syrup has a high-sugar content and generally should be avoided. However, for an occasional party or special occasion it could be used once in a while.

## Oil

*For regular use*
unrefined or cold-pressed corn oil, roasted sesame oil and sesame oil

*For frequent use*
unrefined or cold-pressed olive, peanut, safflower, soya bean and sunflower oils

*To avoid*
butter, cocoa oil, lard, margarine, palm oil, refined and chemically processed vegetable oils

Our bodily requirement for oil (or fat as it is called when solid) is really quite low. In a natural diet most foods contain some oil and seeds, nuts and beans are particularly high in oil. Over and above this a small quantity of oil is needed by most people — say about one teaspoon every day or other day. In recent years there has been a big shift from using saturated animal fats, like butter and lard, to using vegetable oils and margarine. However scientific research has cast doubt on whether unsaturated oils are really so much better than saturated fats. The most important thing is the *quantity* of oils eaten — a teaspoon a day is really plenty for practically everyone living in a temperate climate. Oil is similar to salt in that a small amount is necessary for health, but a lot can be damaging to our health.

The best quality of oil to use is *unrefined* or *cold-pressed* oil, which has been through the minimum of processing and so retains vitamin C and minerals. Refined oils and margarine are solvent-extracted at a high temperature, bleached and chemically treated to make them odorless and have an extremely long shelf life. Besides being loaded with chemicals, they are stripped of their minerals and vitamins.

Oils are used most often in frying or sautéeing vegetable, grain and noodle dishes. For this it is useful to use a brush to lightly oil the bottom of the pan. Occasionally grains, vegetables and fish can also be deep-fried. Tempura (the Japanese term for deep-fried food in batter) is a delicious way of cooking vegetables from time to time. Oil can also be used in dressings for vegetables and salads. For this it is best to heat the oil first — raw oil is very yin and heating it makes it a bit more yang and more digestible.

This chapter may seem to contain a great deal of information to take in in one go. However, what has been described is an *ideal* way of eating. It is best to make gradual changes in your diet, rather than big, sudden ones, to give time for the body and mind to adapt to digesting, assimilating and metabolizing new foods.

# 3. COOKING BALANCED MEALS

In the last chapter we looked at *what* to eat. Now we shall look at *how* to prepare these foods to create meals that are balanced, nutritious and satisfying. Cooking is really like alchemy. You take some basic foods, each with its own unique tastes and energies and using the elements of cooking, transform these basic qualities to increase the flavour and vitality of the food.

| YANG ELEMENTS | YIN ELEMENTS |
|---|---|
| longer cooking (more heat) | shorter or no cooking (less heat) |
| pressure cooking | open cooking e.g. boiling, steaming |
| using little or no water | using more water |
| use of salt and salty seasonings | use of vinegar, lemon juice, mustard and other yin seasonings |
| cutting vegetables into large pieces | cutting vegetables finely |
| use of oil in frying and deep frying[1] | fermentation, e.g. of beverages and pickles |

**Yang and Yin Elements used in Cooking**

1. Although oil is more yin than water, oil reaches a much higher temperature, and so foods cooked in oil are heated more thoroughly.

## YIN AND YANG ELEMENTS IN COOKING

Certain elements used in cooking make foods more contracted, warming and yang, while others make foods more expansive, cooling and yin. These elements are shown in the chart above.

Using these guidelines we can arrange the most commonly used cooking methods or styles on a scale from yang to yin:

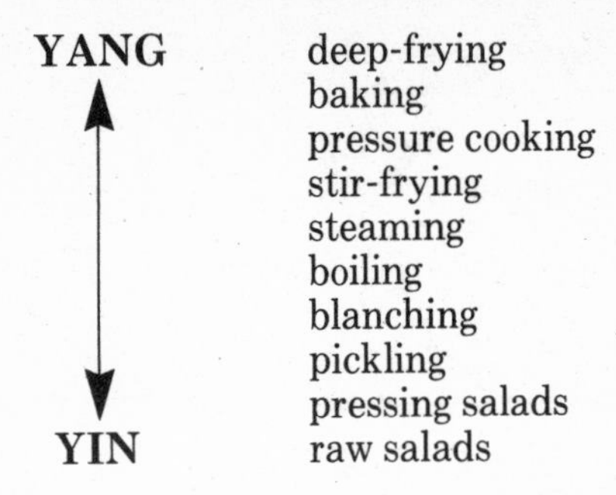


How do we make use of this knowledge of the yin and yang elements and cooking methods? Firstly, we can make our *daily cooking* more balanced by using the more balanced cooking methods more often — pressure cooking, stir-frying, steaming, boiling and blanching — and using the more extreme methods less often or in smaller amounts — deep-frying, baking, pickling, pressing salads and raw salads. Secondly, *within one meal* we can have some more yang dishes — longer cooked, saltier etc and some more yin dishes — lighter cooked, pickled or raw with yin seasonings etc. When there is this polarity within an overall balance, meals tend to be visually attractive, tasty and satisfying. Thirdly, we can create a dynamic balance *within one dish* by using yin and yang elements. For example, some lemon juice or vinegar can bring fish 'alive', roasted seeds or nuts go very well with rice and to make an exciting salad dressing we can use shoyu (yang) and vinegar (yin) or miso (yang) with tahini and lemon juice (yin).

## TYPES OF HEAT USED IN COOKING

Almost everyone will agree that different fuels used for cooking foods produce different tastes and qualities in the foods. These fuels can be arranged on a scale according to whether their effect on foods is more yang or more yin:

wood
charcoal
coal
gas
electricity
microwaves

Any of the more yang types of heat from wood to gas produce a healthy balance in the body. Electric cooking over a long period of time can have a weakening or yin effect on health. Although this is quite a minor consideration, if you do have the choice we would highly recommend that you use gas, coal or wood for your regular cooking. Microwave cooking, the most recently invented and most artificial method of cooking food, is not recommended as a sole or regular source of heat, though occasional use is not going to have such a great effect on our health.

## THE QUALITY OF YOUR WATER

More water is used in cooking than any other ingredient, so we should not forget about its quality. You may be lucky enough to be supplied with spring or well water, but as this is not the case for most people other means must be found to ensure a pure and chemical-free water supply. Try using a jug with a charcoal based filter inside. There are now several different makes widely available in the shops. I would recommend using one for *all* the water used in cooking.

## COOKING FOR ONE

If you are just cooking for yourself, it is still possible to make balanced, nutritious and appetizing meals without spending hours in the kitchen. Whole grains and beans take the longest time to cook, so always prepare a large pot of each at any one time. You can use them freshly cooked for your first meal and then use them as the basis of other meals over the next few days. Cooked whole grains like rice, barley and millet will generally keep for 1 or 2 days in a cool part of your kitchen, covered loosely with a mat or cloth (they tend to become hard and tasteless if kept in a refrigerator). Cooked beans can be stored in a similar way or in a refrigerator. For your next few meals the grains can be warmed by steaming, frying with some vegetables, pressing with beans into burgers and then frying, or mixing with vegetables, nuts, etc to make a rice salad. Beans can be warmed with a little water in a saucepan, cooked with vegetables to make a fresh dish, mashed to make a spread or filling or used as the basis of a bean and vegetable soup.

Quicker meals can be created with noodles, bulghur wheat, couscous, bread, tofu, tempeh and fish. For snacks, always have some rice cakes, roasted seeds or nuts and crackers handy in the kitchen. You can, of course, snack on left-over dishes from your last meal.

## COOKING FOR CHILDREN

Children are often more interested in the sweets and snacks they are used to and are usually very aware of what their friends are eating. They probably won't understand the good sense in eating more whole, natural and balanced foods. Forcing them to eat better foods will only lead to their rejection of them. Rather encouragement is needed. If they see you regularly eating new healthier foods, curiosity will get the better of them after a time and they will probably want to start trying some of them themselves.

It can also help a great deal to make foods that are exciting to look at — lots of different shapes, colours, textures, sizes etc. They usually like 'finger-food' or food that comes in small 'packets' like noodles (lots of different shapes are available to try), burgers, sushi, stuffed pita bread, biscuits and so on.

Children's tastes and needs are also a little different from adults' tastes and needs. They are smaller and more compact and active or yang. To balance their condition they therefore need a more yin diet. Small children (under 6 or 7 years) need very little salt, so avoid giving them salty dishes and snacks. They also need more sweet-tasting foods, such as cooked sweet vegetables like onions, parsnips, broccoli and cauliflower and good quality desserts made with fresh or dried chestnuts, barley malt, rice syrup, concentrated apple juice and fresh and dried fruits.

# 4.
# IN THE KITCHEN

## ORGANIZING YOUR KITCHEN

In recent years kitchens have tended to become smaller and smaller. It is as if the kitchen was the *least* important room in a house, when it is actually the *most* important, being the place where the health of the household is created. Whether your kitchen is large or small, make it a place that is a pleasure to work in and where you can smoothly and efficiently produce attractive, appetizing and healthy meals. It helps to organize it well, with foods and cooking utensils stored close at hand in an orderly way, so that you always know where to find them. Also keep it as clean and free from clutter as possible, so that you can approach your cooking with a clear mind.

## WHERE TO SHOP

If you are unfamiliar with some of the foods used in this book, you may need to explore some different shops. Generally most of these foods can be obtained in a good wholefood or health food shop. Delicatessens can also be useful sources of some of the foods and even supermarkets are now stocking many of them. If you have a Chinese food shop near you, it could also be worth having a look in.

Compare prices in different shops as they will probably vary widely. Wholefood shops are often cheaper than health food shops. They may also sell some foods in larger quantities at a discount. However don't always go for the cheapest foods, as they may be of inferior quality. If you have any problems obtaining particular foods, a list of mail order suppliers is given in the Appendix on page 160. You could also mention them to your local shop — it may be interested in stocking them too.

## BASIC INGREDIENTS

If you decide that you are going to use the recipes in this book regularly, then it makes sense to stock up on all the main ingredients. Nearly all of these foods store very well, which means that you can stock up on them once a fortnight or even once a month, and only need to shop for fresh vegetables and fruits more frequently. Try to keep a good supply of the following:

*Grains*
Short or medium grain brown rice, barley, wheat, millet, rolled oats, couscous, wholewheat spaghetti and noodles, pitta bread, rice cakes

*Beans and bean products*
Aduki beans, green or brown lentils, chick peas, kidney beans, split peas, tofu in the refrigerator, tempeh in the freezer

*Sea vegetables*
Wakame, kombu or kelp, arame, hiziki, nori, agar agar

*Seeds and nuts*
Sesame, pumpkin and sunflower seeds, almonds, peanuts, walnuts, dried chestnuts

*Dried fruits*
Sultanas, raisins, pears, apricots, apple rings

*Seasonings and condiments*
Miso, shoyu soy sauce, rice or cider vinegar, mustard, root ginger, umeboshi plums, sesame oil, sesame spread or tahini

*Natural sweeteners*
Barley malt, rice syrup, concentrated apple juice

*Beverages*
Three-year twig tea (Bancha or Kukicha), grain coffee, apple juice, spring or well water

The best way of storing most of these foods is in glass jars. This keeps them clean and dry and you can always see how much you have got left. Glass is easy to clean and adds no odours of its own to foods. A few foods are best kept in the refrigerator. Tempeh can be kept frozen for several weeks or months and tofu must be kept cool. If you get through your jar or packet of miso slowly, it could be an idea to keep that in the refrigerator too. In the heat of summer salad vegetables could be stored in the refrigerator, if you cannot buy them fresh every day. Try not to put left-overs in the refrigerator, as they loose some of their flavour and vitality. They are best kept in a cool place, although in very hot weather refrigeration may be necessary rather than letting them go off and wasting food.

## COOKING UTENSILS

You may find that in time you need to get some new utensils for your kitchen. The most important thing is to have a good set of saucepans that you like and feel comfortable using. I prefer stainless steel and enamelled saucepans and cast iron frying pans. Glass and stoneware are also fine to use, but avoid aluminium and non-stick coated pans, as these materials tend to get scraped off and you end up eating them as well. A pressure cooker is invaluable too for cooking grains and certain beans, but again make sure to get one made of stainless steel rather than aluminium. A wok can be a useful addition for frying vegetables Chinese style.

Good sharp knives are essential for cutting vegetables — Japanese or Chinese style knives made of carbon or stainless steel are ideal. A stiff-bristled brush is useful for scrubbing vegetables clean of soil. A fine grater can be used for grating root ringer, lemon rind and other foods. A wire mesh sieve will be used often for washing grains, beans and seeds. A stainless steel or bamboo steamer is a useful item for steaming vegetables and for reheating rice and other grain dishes.

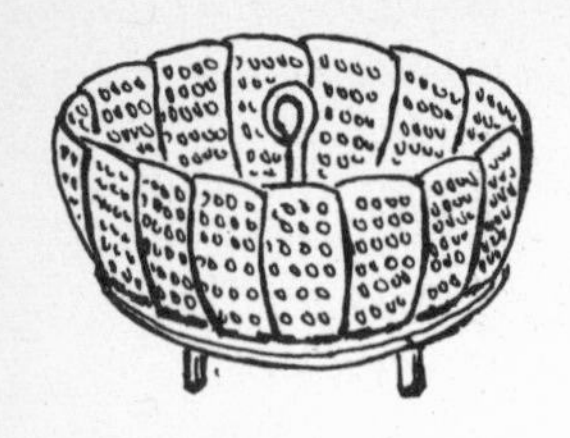

Stainless Steel Steamer.

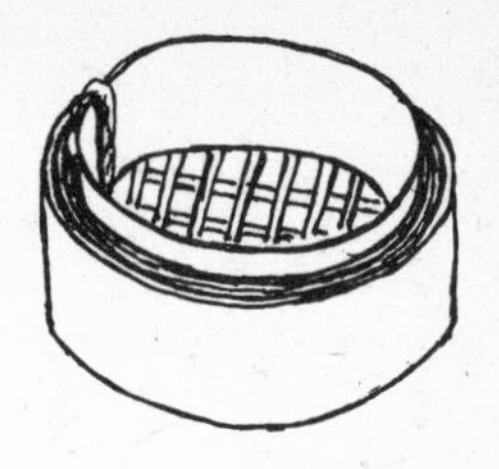

Bamboo Steamer.

Try using a Japanese pestle and mortar, called a *suribachi* for grinding seeds and nuts, making purées, mashing beans etc. It has fine lines scored on the inside which makes grinding quick and easy. The odd electrical appliance may also help. A coffee grinder makes quick work of grinding seeds and nuts to a fine powder for dressings and a blender is sometimes useful for creating creamy soups, dips and desserts.

Suribachi.

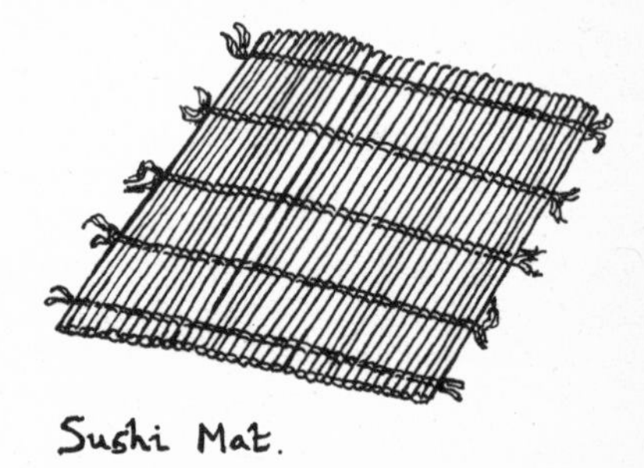

Sushi Mat.

A *sushi mat* for making the Japanese speciality sushi can also be useful. Sushi are rolls of rice or noodles wrapped in flat sheets of nori (sea vegetable — see page 19) with pickles, fish and other ingredients in the centre. If you cannot obtain a genuine sushi mat, any small piece of bamboo mat will do just as well.

# 5.
# VEGETABLE CUTTING

The preparation and cutting of vegetables forms an important part of a yin-yang balanced diet. When meat or dairy foods are the principle part of a meal, the vegetable dishes can be kept quite simple. With meals centred around grains, beans and vegetables, we need to develop a much wider variety of preparing and cooking vegetables. Using different cutting styles is one way to do this. There is an almost infinite number of ways of cutting different vegetables. Below are the styles that I use most often. These styles enhance the natural energy, appearance and flavour of particular vegetables and create most attractive and appetizing meals.

It is essential to have a moderately large and very sharp knife that cuts vegetables cleanly and easily. I use a stainless steel Japanese model with a rectangular blade 7 inches long and 1½ inches deep. It is sharpened regularly on a wet stone to keep cutting easy and effective. Cutting vegetables is a real art and needs to be approached as such. Use a large wooden chopping board, relax and give yourself plenty of room. Hold the vegetable in one hand with the fingertips tucked under the knuckles for safety's sake. With the knife in the other hand, bring the tip to the vegetable and slice forward and downwards, so that you use the whole of the length of the blade. The stroke should be smooth, fluid and natural. Avoid sawing or chopping straight down on the vegetables.

These are two main points to think about when cutting vegetables. Firstly, use a variety of styles in one meal to create dishes with quite different appearances and textures. Secondly, think of how long you want to cook the vegetable. If you are cooking it a long time, cut it into large pieces. If you are cooking it for a shorter time, cut it into smaller and finer pieces. Also, cut all the pieces the same size, so that they will all be cooked the same amount. Finally, treat your vegetables with respect at all times. Their living energy will soon be yours, so handle them with loving care all through your cooking.

## CUTTING STYLES

Here are the cutting styles. They may seem slow and difficult at first, but with time you can become very quick and accurate.

**Rounds**
Hold the knife at right-angles to the vegetable and cut straight across as thick as required.

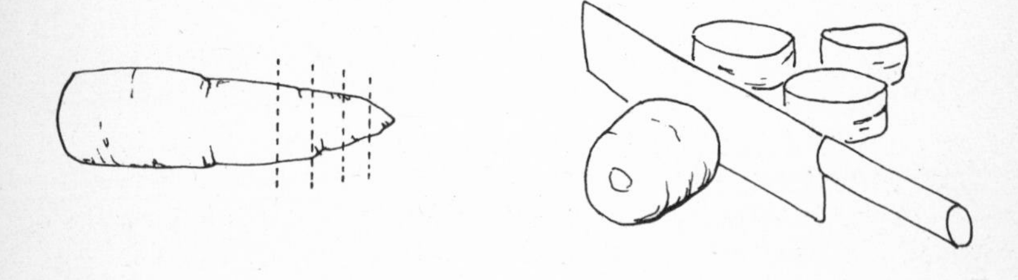

**Diagonal slices**
Hold the knife at an angle to the vegetable and make diagonal cuts as thick as needed. The angle of the knife determines the length of the pieces.

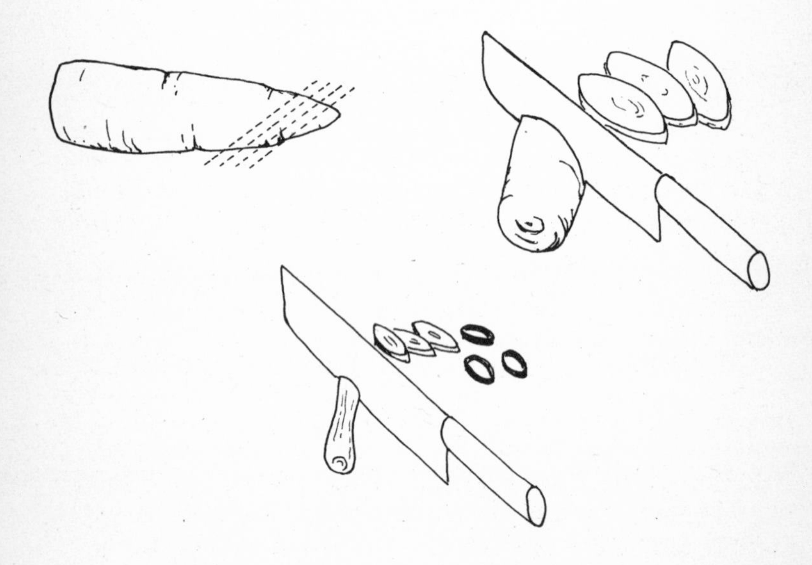

## Matchsticks

Cut diagonal slices (see above), then cut the slices lengthways into matchstick shaped pieces.

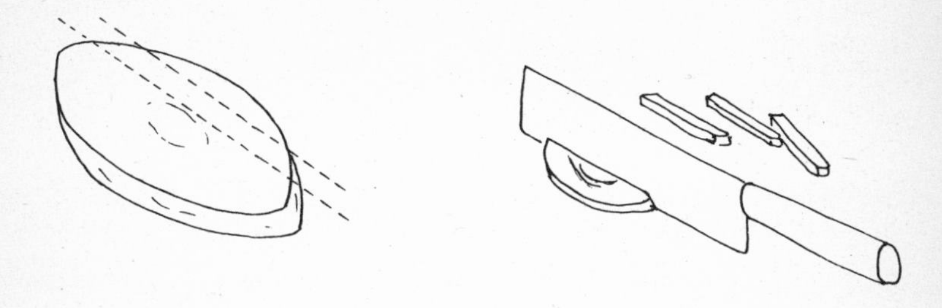

## Irregular chunks

Cut the vegetable on the diagonal, turn the vegetable a quarter turn towards you, then cut on the diagonal again.

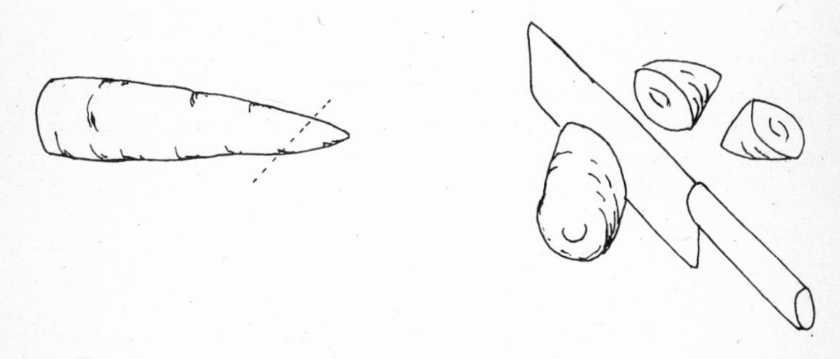

## Dicing

Cut the vegetable in half lengthways. Take a half and cut into lengthways slices. Lay the half down keeping its slices together and cut across to form cubes.

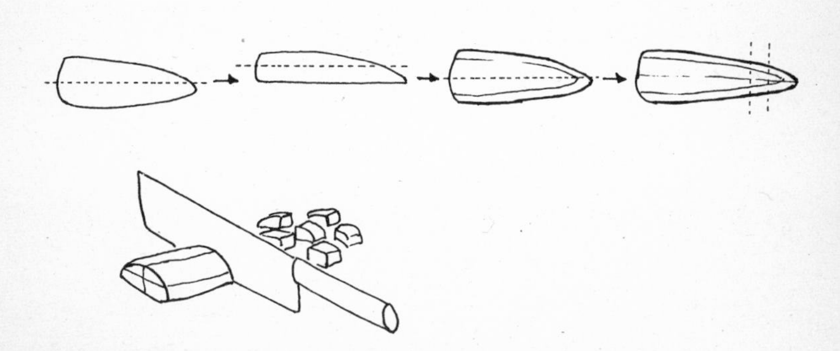

## Dicing onions

Trim the top and bottom off the onion and peel it. Cut the onion in half vertically. Lay a half flat side down and cut lengthways. Then cut across to form cubes.

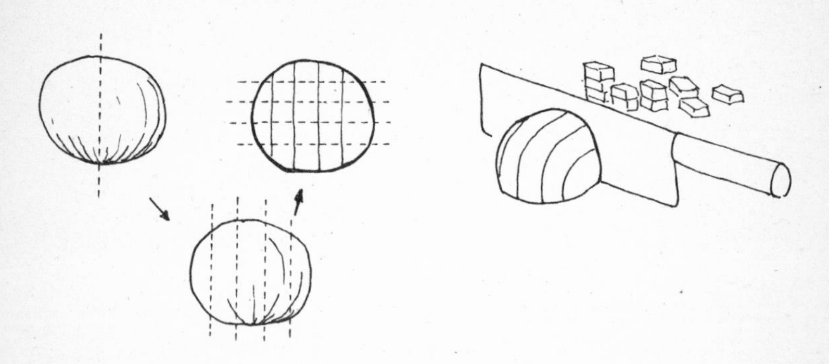

## Half moons

Cut the vegetable in half lengthways. Lay a half down and cut straight across as thick as required.

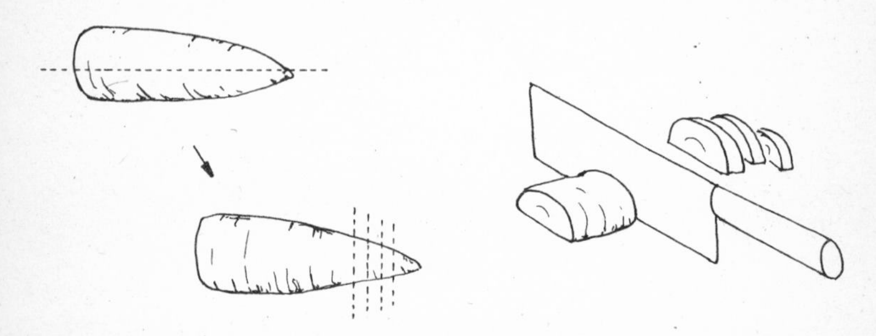

## Onion half moons

Trim the top and bottom off the onion and peel it. Cut the onion in half vertically. Lay a half flat side down and make lengthways slices close together.

**Flowers**
Cut four or five grooves along the length of the vegetable. With a long root vegetable, first cut it into two or three inch lengths. Then slice the vegetable into thin rounds.

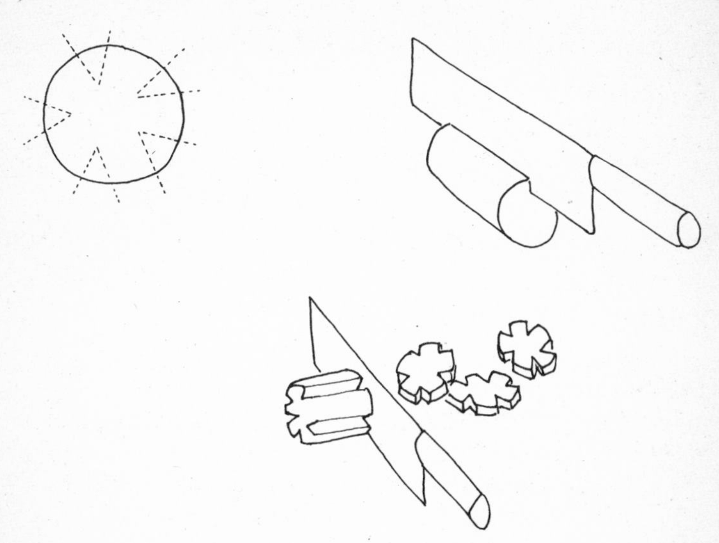

**Slicing leaves**
Cut each leaf in half through the centre spine. Stack several halves on top of each other and cut diagonally into strips ⅛ to ¼ inch wide.

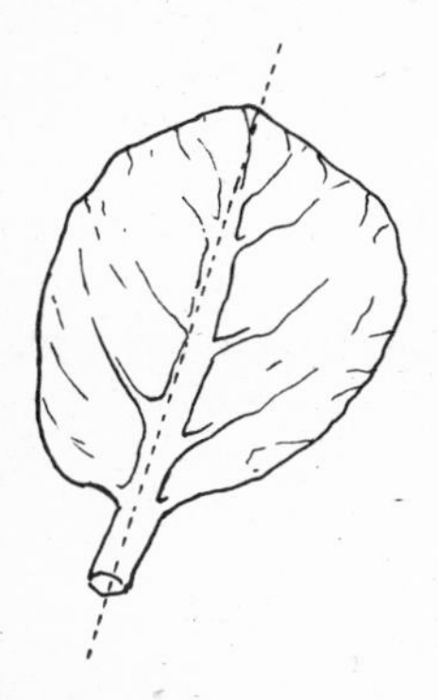

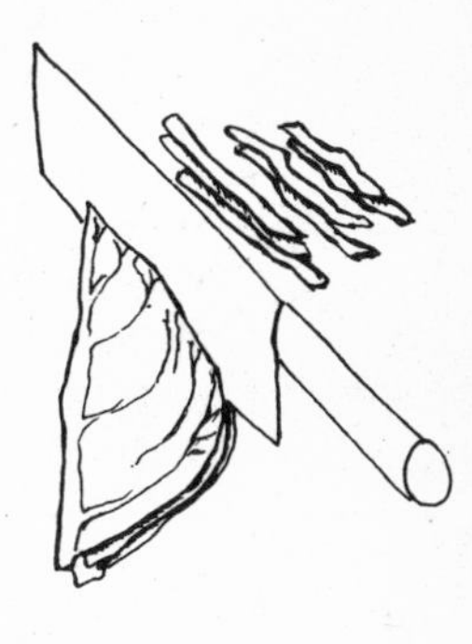

# 6. PLANNING MEALS

## GENERAL GUIDELINES

Most people will be used to having a meat, egg or cheese dish as the centre of a meal, with fairly simple vegetable dishes to go with it. In a yin-yang balanced diet, a grain, vegetable or fish dish usually forms the central part of a meal, with more varied and interesting vegetable dishes providing a range of tastes, energies and nutrients. So in planning your menu, start by thinking of the grain, bean, bean product or fish dish, then choose vegetable dishes that complement and harmonize with it. Be prepared to spend a little longer than you may be used to for preparing the accompanying vegetable dishes.

In planning meals remember the ideal proportions of the principle foods (see pages 16 to 21) to eat each day — whole grains 35-50 per cent, vegetables 25-35 per cent, beans and bean products 5-10 per cent, sea vegetables 3-4 per cent and fermented foods (including soups seasoned with miso and shoyu and pickles) around 5 per cent. These are supplemented by secondary foods such as fish and seafood, fruit, seeds and nuts, various seasonings, condiments, sweeteners and beverages. It is not necessary to eat all of the principle foods at every meal, as long as they are eaten in approximately these proportions over one day, so don't worry too much if the odd day's eating misses something out — the ideal proportions are meant as a general guideline, not as a rigid rule.

For lunch it isn't always necessary to have a high-protein food. Leftover grain from the night before, such as rice, bulghur wheat or millet, can be reheated in some tasty and satisfying way such as steaming, frying, rolling into balls or cooking with some finely chopped vegetables and a variety of seasonings. Some freshly steamed, boiled or sautéed vegetables can then complete the meal. To make a quick meal from scratch, wholewheat pasta, couscous and bulghur wheat are quick to cook.

At supper time a richer and more varied meal is generally required. The main course should generally include a whole grain, a high-protein food such as beans, tempeh, tofu or fish and a variety of vegetables. Sea vegetables can be used in a soup and with any bean dish or perhaps as a separate vegetable. With fish serve a generous helping of boiled, pressed or raw salad, dressed and decoratively garnished to balance the yang animal food. Try to avoid eating meat, although occasionally a small amount of chicken or egg can be used to advantage.

At first preparing balanced and varied meals may take you a long time because of new and unfamiliar ingredients and cooking methods but take it at a steady pace so that you can enjoy your new way of cooking and eating. After a while it will become as natural to you as your previous way of eating. A good tip is to always cook enough whole grains and beans to provide for more than one meal. That way they can be used for the meal at hand, with enough left over to form the basis of a quickly prepared meal later. For example, if you cook a rice or millet dish for supper, cook enough for lunch next day. They can be quickly steamed or fried or incorporated into a new dish. Many of the recipes in this book are designed for six people — if you are smaller in number then you can still use the same quantities and be left with some for another meal. You can also minimise the time you spend preparing a meal by beginning with the preparation of the dishes needing the longest cooking. These are usually bean or whole grain dishes. Once these are on, go on to the dishes needing the next longest cooking — maybe a long-cooked vegetable dish or a pressed salad. End up by making quickly prepared dishes, so that all the dishes are ready at approximately the same time. With practice you will find that you can greatly shorten the time needed to cook a meal.

## MENU PLANS

Below are menu plans for one week. These are intended to give general guidelines for planning nutritionally and energetically balanced meals.

**Breakfast**
*Sourdough pancakes* (see page 74) with hot barley malt and roasted sunflower seeds
**Lunch**
*French onion soup with tempura croutons* (see page 50)
*Couscous loaf* (see page 65)
*Kinpira carrots* (see page 106)
*Greens rolls* (see page 113)
**Supper**
*Rice, sweet rice and chestnuts* (see page 56)
*Nishime carrots and yellow turnips* (see page 98)
*Cabbage and watercress salad* (see page 117)
*Brine pickles* (see page 132)
*Apple and raisin crumble* (see page 144)

**Breakfast**
Oat flake porridge made with water and a pinch of sea salt with *Gomasio* (see page 136)
*Grated carrot and parsley saute* (see page 102) with rice syrup
**Lunch**
Pitta bread filled with *Tofu spread* (see page 142) or *Sunset dip* (see page 141)
*Carrot, broccoli and red radish boiled salad* (see page 115)
**Supper**
*Cream of carrot and onion soup* (see page 49)
Short grain rice mixed with sesame seeds
*Deep-fried stuffed seitan* (see page 79) with *Ginger shoyu dip sauce* (see page 130)
*Baked pumpkin or swede* (see page 108)
*Greens rolls* (see page 113)
*Baked pear and ginger sauce* (see page 149)

**Breakfast**
Plain millet seasoned with miso and ginger rolled into balls. Serve as they are or with a barley malt and kuzu sauce.
**Lunch**
*Rice sushi* (see *Noodle sushi* variations on page 72)
*Cabbage d'Alsace* (see page 111)
*Onion miso quick pickles* (see page 133)

**Supper**
*Deep fried millet balls* (see page 62)
*Chick pea el rondo* (see page 84)
*Carrot chunks in miso and ginger* (see page 97)
*Spring greens and sunflower seed salad* (see page 116)

**Breakfast**
Plain couscous mixed with roasted and ground sesame seeds with hot rice syrup
**Lunch**
*Split pea and miso soup* (see page 50)
Pitta bread with *Pumpkin seed spread* (see page 128) and slices of cucumber
*Deep fried tempeh* (see page 80) with *Mustard and miso dressing* (see page 131)
**Supper**
*Rice croquettes* (see page 56)
*Aduki beans, kombu and squash* (see page 85)
White cabbage and spring onion raw salad with *Sesame, rice vinegar and umeboshi dressing* (see page 129)
Sauerkraut
*Hazlenut and ginger cookies* (see page 149)

**Breakfast**
Rice flake gallettes — make a thick porridge with rice flakes, water and a little umeboshi, shape it into small patties and toast under the grill until crisp and brown on top. Add hot rice syrup if desired.
**Lunch**
*Couscous salad* (see page 66)
*Nishime carrots and brussels sprouts* (see page 98)
*Red radish and cucumber pressed salad* (see page 120)
**Supper**
*Deep fried cod with green pepper dressing* (see page 91)
*Couscous loaf* (see page 65)
*Carrot and cucumber salad* (see page 120)
*Dandelion coffee mousse with sesame cream* (see page 147)

**Breakfast**
Oatflake porridge made with water and a pinch of sea salt, cooked with raisins and barley malt
Rice cakes with *Pumpkin seed spread* (see page 128) or *Onion butter* (see page 98)
**Lunch**
Sautéed rice, carrot matchsticks, onion half moons and spring

onions with roasted sesame seeds
*Brine pickles* (see page 132)
**Supper**
*Carrot and kombu miso soup with puffed mochi croutons* (see page 51)
*Millet and lentil burgers* (see page 60)
*Baked onions stuffed with sesame couscous* (see page 104)
*Sweet 'n' sour carrots* (see page 110)
Steamed leeks or cabbage

**Breakfast**
*Scrambled tofu* (see page 90) with plain couscous or wholemeal toast
**Lunch**
Fried buckwheat or wholewheat noodles
*Tempeh with onions, kombu and umeboshi* (see page 81)
Boiled broccoli
**Supper**
*Chinese cabbage rolls* (see page 51)
*Sole marinade* (see page 96)
*Millet and almond pasta rolls* (see page 63)
*Swede and carrot sticks* (see page 101)
Boiled mange tout
*Apricot and cherry pie* (see page 151)

# 7. SOUPS AND STARTERS

### Cream of Carrot and Onion Soup

Serves 6.

*6 medium carrots, 6 medium onions, 225 g/8 oz rice flakes, 110 g/ 4 oz dulse, 1 tablespoon barley miso, 1 tablespoon umeboshi paste, 30 g/1 oz finely chopped parsley, 2¼ litres/4 pt water*

Wash and cut the carrots finely on the diagonal (see page 40). Dice the onions finely. Bring the water to a boil and add the onions. When the onions are transparent, add the carrots and dulse, then cover and simmer gently for 10 to 15 minutes. Add the rice flakes and turn the heat down very low. Simmer the soup gently for 20 to 30 minutes.

Mix the miso with a little vegetable cooking water to make a smooth runny paste. In a separate bowl mix the umeboshi paste with a little vegetable cooking water again to form a smooth runny paste. Stir this umeboshi paste mixture into the soup.

Purée the soup in a blender and return it to the saucepan. It turns a lovely golden colour when puréed. Add the finely chopped parsley and the miso paste and cook for a further 5 minutes. Serve the soup, sprinkling a spoonful of raw chopped parsley on top of each bowl.

*Variations:* In season pumpkin can be used instead of carrot. Leek can be used instead of onion. Carrot and broccoli makes an interesting alternative. For a richer soup, sauté the vegetables first in sesame oil.

*Serving suggestions:* This soup can be served with a decoration of carrot flowers (see page 43) or a little finely cut leek sautéed with umeboshi vinegar. Croûtons are an attractive addition for a nice crunchy soup. For children chunks of cucumber can go down well. Roasted and slithered almonds also make a decorative garnish.

## French Onion Soup with Tempura Croûtons

Serves 6.

*140 g/5 oz strong white flour or wholewheat pastry flour, 280 g/10 oz brown rice flour, 1 teaspoon kuzu, 1 to 2 pinches sea salt, 3 medium carrots, sesame or sunflower oil for deep-frying, 6 medium onions, 3 tablespoons sesame oil, 1 teaspoon dried thyme, 2 litres/3½ pt water, 5 tablespoons shoyu*

Make the batter by mixing the flours, powdered kuzu and salt together. Add enough water to make a thin batter consistency and leave it to sit for at least half an hour before using.

Wash and cut the carrots into 1 cm/½ inch chunks. Pour 5 to 7½ cm/2 to 3 inches of oil into a saucepan and heat until a piece of carrot dropped into the oil quickly rises to the surface. Dip the carrot chunks in the batter and deep-fry, 3 or 4 at a time, for 3 to 4 minutes, until they are crisp. Take these tempura carrot croûtons out with a slotted spoon and drain them on kitchen towel. Keep the oil for the next time you deep-fry. Place the croûtons on a serving dish, so people can help themselves as they eat their soup.

Wash and cut the onions into fine half moons (see page 42). Using a heavy-bottomed saucepan, heat the sesame oil. When the oil is hot but not smoking add the onions and sauté them for 10 minutes until they are soft and succulent. Add the water and thyme and simmer gently for 20 minutes, then add the shoyu. Let the soup stand for a few minutes to let the flavour of the shoyu blend in, then serve with the tempura carrot croûtons.

*Variations:* The addition of ginger or spring onions instead of the thyme makes a pleasant variant to the soup. French onion soup served with thyme and without the croûtons makes a lovely first course for a fish meal — the croûtons can be a little oily to serve with fish. Other *Tempura vegetables* (see page 108) work well as croûtons for this soup and cauliflower florets are very attractive.

## Split Pea and Miso Soup

Serves 6.

*170 g/6 oz green split peas, 60 g/2 oz arame sea vegetable, 3½ litres/6 pt water, 2 onions, finely diced, 2 carrots, cut in fine matchsticks, 2 tablespoons of barley miso, watercress to garnish*

Wash and soak the split peas in 850 ml/1½ pt water for 4 hours. This shortens the cooking time and makes the peas more digestible. Rinse the arame in a sieve. Place the arame on the bottom of a saucepan and the split peas on top. Add all the water and simmer for 40 minutes, then add the carrots and onions and simmer for 15 minutes. Blend the miso in a little water and add it to the soup. Garnish with watercress and serve.

*Note:* This soup is delightful for people who like a sweet-tasting soup. It goes well with many foods and is a good appetizer.

## Carrot and Kombu Miso Soup with Puffed Mochi Croûtons

*Serves 6.*

*4 medium carrots, 15 cm/6 inch strip of kombu, 2½ litres/4½ pt water, 6 medium florets of cauliflower, small piece ginger root, 1 packet dried mochi*

Soak the kombu in water for half an hour and then cut it into very fine squares. Wash and cut the carrots into fine julienne strips. Bring the water to a boil and add first the kombu, then the carrots. Turn the heat to low and gently simmer for 15 minutes, then add the cauliflower florets and simmer 2 or 3 minutes more. Blend the miso to a paste with a little of the vegetable water and add to the soup. Simmer very gently for 2 minutes. Grate the fresh ginger root and squeeze 1 teaspoon of juice into the soup, then cook for a further minute. Remove from the heat.

Cut a third to a half of the packet of dried mochi into 1 cm/½ inch cubes or triangles. Place the mochi cubes on a baking tray and grill them on a medium setting for about 3 minutes on the first side and 1 to 2 minutes more on the other side. The mochi should puff up and turn crisp and golden.

Gently reheat the soup and serve with a few mochi croûtons sprinkled on top of each bowl.

*Variations:* The mochi squares could be pan-fried, either dry or with a little sesame oil or can be deep-fried. Serve them immediately while hot with the soup. These mochi croûtons can also brighten up a rice risotto or a vegetable stew.

## Chinese Cabbage Rolls

Serves 6.

*3 large carrots, ½ cucumber, 150 ml/¼ pt umeboshi vinegar, 150 ml/¼ pt rice vinegar, 570 ml/1 pt water, 2 medium Chinese cabbages, 1 pinch of sea salt*

Wash and grate the carrots and cucumber and marinate for at least 1 hour in a mixture of the umeboshi vinegar and rice vinegar.

Wash the outer green leaves of the Chinese cabbages separately and with a V-shaped nick cut out the thickest part of the stalk, so that they roll easily. Heat the water and add a pinch of sea salt. Blanch the Chinese cabbage leaves individually for little under a minute, then spread them out to drain and dry a little.

Lay a sushi mat out on a chopping board and lay the Chinese cabbage leaves alternately up and down and across the mat. Cover the whole mat with two layers of Chinese cabbage leaves. Roll the mat up gently around the leaves and squeeze out the excess liquid into a bowl to use for soup stock. Unroll the sushi mat and gently spread out the leaves on the mat again.

Drain the carrot and cucumber by placing in a sieve. Save the marinade as a dressing for a raw or blanched salad.

Make a 2.5 cm/1 inch high line of the carrot and cucumber a third of the way down the length of the cabbage leaves. Roll the leaves up with the sushi mat, pulling back the edge of the mat so that it doesn't get caught up in the roll. As you roll press the cabbage leaves firmly together to make a compact roll that sticks together well. When the leaves are completely rolled up, wrap the sushi mat around the roll and squeeze gently but firmly to make the roll stick together. Unwrap the roll and cut into 5 or 6 pieces. They look very decorative served with a few sprigs of parsley or a wedge of lemon. This is a very good low calorie starter for people wanting to slim.

*Variations:* Spring greens or soft outer cabbage leaves can be used if Chinese cabbages are not in season, but the delicacy and transparent attractiveness of Chinese cabbage rolls makes them particularly appropriate as an appetizer.

*Serving suggestions:* Chinese cabbage rolls are an excellent accompaniment for a fish dish — particularly whole grilled fish such as *Sole marinade* (see page 96).

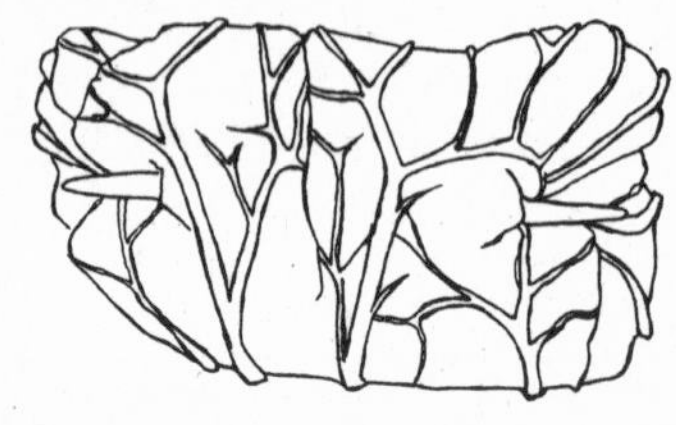

**Corn on the Cob**

Serves 6.

*6 fresh (or frozen) corn cobs, 1 litre/2 pt water, 2 pinches of sea salt, 225 g/8 oz pumpkin seeds, 290 ml/½ pt umeboshi vinegar*

Using a large saucepan bring the water to a boil. Wash the corn cobs. Add the sea salt to the boiling water then the corn cobs. Simmer the cobs on a gentle heat for 20 minutes. Remove the cobs and drain them under cool running water in a sieve. This brightens the colour of the corn to a vivid yellow.

Wash the pumpkin seeds and drain them. Dry roast in a frying pan until they pop. Blend the seeds to a powder in a coffee grinder or suribachi and mix with the umeboshi vinegar. Serve this as a dressing for the corn in a separate bowl.

## Carrot Juice

Serves 6.

*6 large carrots, 2 litres/3½ pt water, 2 pinches of sea salt*

Wash and grate the carrots. Place in a liquidizer with the water and sea salt and blend until it is smooth and creamy.

*Serving suggestions:* This carrot juice is delightful served cold in glasses with a twist of lemon or hot in small hand bowls with some mochi croûtons (see *Carrot and kombu soup with puffed mochi croûtons* on page 51) or a little pinch of thyme or chopped parsley for garnish.

## Pickled Onions with Red Cabbage Salad

Serves 6.

*570 ml/1 pt water, 15 cm/6 inch strip of kombu, 450 g/1 lb round pickling onions, 225 g/8 oz red cabbage, 290 ml/½ pt umeboshi vinegar, 290 ml/½ pt sauerkraut juice*

Bring water to a boil and add the kombu sea vegetable. Peel the onions then blanch in the boiling water for little less than a minute. Remove the onions with a slotted spoon and place them in a bowl.

Wash and cut the red cabbage into very fine 2.5 cm/1 inch long shreds. Blanch the cabbage in the boiling water for 1 minute and remove it with a slotted spoon. Rinse the cabbage in a sieve under gently running cold water. This brings out the crispness, colour and flavour of the cabbage. Drain the cabbage and place it in a large flat bowl. Put the pickling onions on top. Mix together the umeboshi vinegar and sauerkraut juice and pour this liberally over the onion and red cabbage. Leave for 2 to 4 hours.

*Serving suggestions:* Serve the onion and red cabbage pickles on a bed of lettuce with a sprig or two of parsley for garnish.

# 8. GRAINS

Looking over the spectrum of grains, rice is the most balanced and therefore I use it most frequently. In a temperate climate the other most appropriate grains are barley, wheat, oats and millet. I tend to use these grains a lot, cooking them with rice or separately in many varied dishes.

Many split grains and grain products are enjoyable to eat and are usually quick to cook. Principle among these are noodles, couscous, bulghur wheat, rice flakes and oat flakes, as well as salt-free crackers and bread. Rice flakes and oat flakes can be used as thickeners for soups and stews and for stuffing vegetables. Flaked grains make good breakfast porridge.

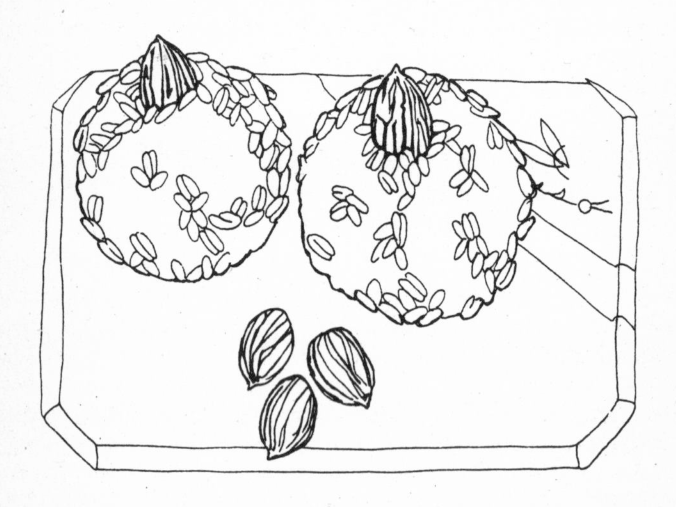

## RICE

Rice should be whole grain brown rice and preferably organic. If rice is organic it tastes much better. Wash rice carefully in a sieve and either pressure cook or boil — pressure cooked rice has a better flavour and is more digestible than boiled rice.

## Pressure Cooked Rice

Serves 4 to 6.

*600 g/1¼ lb short or medium grain brown rice, 1 litre/2 pt water, 3 pinches sea salt*

Wash the rice and place in the pressure cooker. Add the water and sea salt. Bring up to pressure on a high heat, then turn the heat low and pressure cook for 7 minutes. Take the pressure cooker off the heat and allow the pressure to come down naturally.

Take the rice out while it is still warm, one spoonful at a time, and gently separate the grains. It is best to keep cooked rice in wood or ceramic containers as they keep its flavour and freshness longer. Glass is also useful and looks attractive.

*Variations:* There are an infinite number of ways to cook rice so that it is always interesting and different. Rice can be cooked with beans. It is particularly delicious when cooked with aduki beans. Boil the aduki beans with a 15 cm/6 inch strip of kombu for 30 to 40 minutes, then add to the washed rice and pressure cook for 7 minutes.

Rice is also good cooked with 20 per cent other grains. Rice and barley, rice and oats, rice and wheat, rice and millet and rice and sweet rice are all delicious combinations. For cooking rice with barley, wheat or oats, soak the grains for at least 4 hours, then mix with the rice and cook as for plain rice.

## Boiled Rice

Serves 4.

*450 g/1 lb short or medium grain brown rice, 1 litre/2 pt water, 2 pinches of sea salt or 1 teaspoon shoyu soy sauce or 1 teaspoon umeboshi paste*

Wash the rice and place it in a heavy-bottomed saucepan with a tight fitting lid. Add the water and sea salt and bring the rice to a boil on a high heat. Turn the heat very low, cover and simmer gently for 50 minutes to 1 hour. To prevent the bottom of the rice scorching you can use a flame tamer in the last 10 to 15 minutes of cooking.

To boil rice for a larger number of people add slightly less water. For example to 675 g/1½ lb rice add 1½ litres/2½ pt water and 3 pinches of sea salt.

## Rice, Sweet Rice and Chestnuts

Serves 6.

*225 g/8 oz short or medium grain brown rice, 225 g/8 oz sweet rice, 170 g/6 oz dried chestnuts, 3 good pinches of sea salt, 2 litres/3½ pt water*

Soak the chestnuts overnight or for at least 4 hours. Wash the rice and sweet rice together in a sieve. Place the two rices together in a pressure cooker and add the chestnuts together with their soaking water. The chestnut soaking water is very sweet and adds a great deal of flavour to the finished dish. Fresh chestnuts, which have been carefully shelled, can be used but are sometimes bitter. Pressure cook the rice and chestnuts as for ordinary rice for 7 minutes.

*Variations:* If sweet rice is not available, you can just cook brown rice and chestnuts. If dried chestnuts are not available, then use aduki beans or black soya beans. Black soya beans are readily available from Chinese supermarkets. Wash and dry roast the black soya beans in a heavy-bottomed frying pan, over a medium flame, for 10 minutes. Make sure the black beans don't scorch or they become bitter. Add the black beans to the washed rice and pressure cook as with plain rice.

## Rice Croquettes

Serves 6.

*340 g/12 oz leftover rice or rice and oats, rice and barley etc, 170 g/6 oz grated carrot, 225 g/8 oz roasted and chopped or ground sunflower seeds, 1½ punnets mustard cress, 1½ tablespoons mugi miso, 2 to 3 tablespoons sesame or toasted sesame oil, 2 teaspoons ginger juice (squeezed from freshly grated ginger)*

Mash the rice slightly in a suribachi and add all the other ingredients except the sesame oil and ginger juice. Rinse your hands lightly under cold running water and shape the mixture into round rissoles.

Heat the sesame oil in a heavy-bottomed frying pan and add the rissoles. Fry for 5 to 10 minutes on either side on a low heat until nicely browned. One or two minutes before the end of cooking sprinkle the ginger juice over the croquettes and serve.

*Variations:* This mixture can also be rolled into log-shaped croquettes and deep-fried. For deep-frying serve with a *Ginger shoyu dip sauce* (see page 130).

*Serving suggestions:* For a light lunch serve with grilled tempeh fingers topped with mustard and steamed greens. For a more substantial dinner serve with *Chick pea el rondo* (see page 84) and boiled cabbage.

## Rice Salad I

Serves 6.

*560 g/1¼ lb short or medium grain brown rice, 1¼ litres/2¼ pt water, 3 pinches sea salt, 2 corn cobs, 225 g/8 oz peanuts, 10 spring onions, cut finely on the diagonal, 170 g/6 oz mange tout, cut into slithers, 225 g/8 oz finely diced carrots, 1 pinch of sea salt, 2 tablespoons tahini, 2 tablespoons rice vinegar, 2 teaspoons umeboshi paste (or 3 umeboshi plums), 290 ml/½ pt water*

Pressure cook or boil the rice as instructed on page 55 and place in a large ceramic or wooden serving bowl. Allow the rice to cool.

Bring 860 ml/1½ pt water to a boil and add the sea salt. Cut the corn from the cob by cutting lengthways down the cob with a sharp knife, rotating the cob through about 60 degrees and again cutting lengthways down the cob. Repeat 5 times. Save the cob for soup stock and cook the corn for 3 minutes. Drain the corn in a sieve and rinse it lightly under cold water. This brings out the flavour and the lovely rich colour of the corn.

Boil the diced carrots for 2 minutes, then drain and rinse in a sieve under cold water. Boil the mange tout for 2 minutes and again rinse under cold water. Wash and dry roast the peanuts under the grill or in a frying pan. Mix the nuts and cooked vegetables with the rice.

Make up a dressing by blending the umeboshi paste and water to a creamy consistency in a suribachi or blender. Add the tahini and blend, then mix in the rice vinegar. Add more water if necessary, to make whatever kind of thick or thin dressing you like. Pour this over the rice and vegetables and leave to stand for at least 30 minutes before serving.

*Serving suggestions:* This dish is nice at a party or picnic served with *Lentil pâté* (see page 85) and steamed greens.

### Rice Salad II

Serves 6.

*560 g/1$^1/_4$ lb short or medium grain brown rice, 1$^1/_4$ litres/2$^1/_4$ pt water, 3 pinches of sea salt, 225 g/8 oz sunflower seeds, 12 round red radishes, 1 cucumber cut into fine half moons, 110 g/4 oz chopped parsley, 2 tablespoons rice vinegar, 1$^1/_2$ tablespoons umeboshi vinegar (or shoyu), 2 tablespoons toasted sesame oil (or pre-heated sesame oil)*

Pressure cook or boil the rice as described on page 55, place in a large bowl and allow to cool.

While the rice is cooking, wash and dry roast the sunflower seeds until they are golden brown. Bring 425 ml/$^3/_4$ pt water to a boil and blanch the whole radishes for a few seconds. Remove the radishes and rinse them under cold running water in a sieve. Cut the radishes into fine slices. Wash and cut the cucumber into fine half moons (see page 42) and mix with the radishes in a bowl. Blend together the umeboshi vinegar and toasted sesame oil with a fork and then mix in the rice vinegar. Pour this dressing over the cucumber and radishes and marinate for at least half an hour.

Drain the radishes and cucumber and mix with the roasted sunflower seeds and parsley. Mix this with the rice and serve.

*Serving suggestions:* This salad goes nicely with a flat fish such as *Sole marinade* (see page 96).

### Rice and Barley with Onions and Sesame Seeds

Serves 6.

*450 g/1 lb short grain rice, 225 g/8 oz pearl barley, 1$^1/_4$ litres/2$^1/_4$ pt water, 3 pinches sea salt, 4 onions cut in thin half moons, 2 teaspoons sesame oil, 110 g/4 oz sesame seeds, 1 teaspoon shoyu*

Wash the barley and soak for 4 hours or overnight in 570 ml/1 pt water.

Wash the rice and place with the barley and barley soaking water in a saucepan. Add the remaining water and the salt and boil for 50 minutes. Then remove into a large serving bowl.

While the rice is cooking, sauté the onions in the oil for 5 minutes or until transparent. Add the shoyu and sauté 5 more minutes, then set aside. Wash and drain the sesame seeds, and dry roast in a frying pan stirring continuously. They are done when they can be easily crushed between the thumb and third finger — they should turn golden but not brown.

Mix the onions and sesame seeds with the cooked rice and barley and serve warm or cold.

## MILLET

Millet is one of the most versatile of the whole grains. It can be used to make vegetable crumbles, to make deep-fried croquettes, as a topping for shepherd's pie, to stuff vegetables and pasta and to make millet loaf. There are many different kinds of millet, each with a unique flavour. Generally I prefer a smaller grained millet with a deep yellow colour for the maximum flavour and energy.

### How to Cook Millet

Wash the millet and dry roast in a frying pan on a medium heat for about 5 minutes. Bring 720 ml/1¼ pt water for every 225 g/8 oz millet to a boil, add a pinch of salt for every 225 g/8 oz millet, and then the millet. Cook on a very low heat for 35 to 40 minutes or until all the water has been absorbed.

### Millet Loaf

Serves 6.

*450 g/1 lb millet, 1½ litres/2½ pt water, 1 pinch of sea salt, 2 tablespoons barley miso, 3 teaspoons ginger juice (squeezed from freshly grated ginger), 4 onions, diced finely, 2 grated carrots, 2 tablespoons sesame oil, 2 tablespoons chives, chopped finely, 170 g/6 oz sunflower seeds*

Wash and dry roast the millet in a frying pan for about 5 minutes until the millet gives off a nutty aroma. Bring the water to a boil, add the onions, and cook for about 5 minutes until they are transparent. Add the millet and sea salt. Turn the heat very low and simmer for 40 minutes. Blend the miso to a smooth paste with a little water and add to the millet. Cook 3 minutes longer and add the ginger juice. Turn off the heat and let the millet sit covered for 2 minutes.

Wash and dry roast the sunflower seeds until they are golden. Heat the sesame oil in a heavy-bottomed frying pan and add the grated carrot. Sauté for 5 minutes on a medium to low heat until the carrot is very sweet tasting.

Mix the carrots in with the millet. Mix in the chives and sunflower seeds, reserving a few for the top of the loaf. Oil a pyrex loaf dish or bread tin and sprinkle the remaining sunflower seeds and chives over the bottom. Spoon in the millet mixture and press it down very firmly. The millet should be in the mould within 20 minutes of finishing cooking, otherwise it doesn't compact well and will break up easily when it is sliced. Cover the mould and chill it for 1 to 2 hours before serving.

*Serving suggestions:* Millet loaf is very versatile and can be used with a *Lentil pâté* (see page 85) or another spread to make sandwiches for children's lunches. It can be served in cubes with a *Pumpkin seed spread* (see page 128) or *Peanut sauce* (see page 129). Millet loaf can be served with a number of dips such as *Sunset dip* (see page 141), *Houmous* (see page 142) or *Tofu spread* (see page 142). The loaf can be baked for 50 minutes and served with tahini and cucumber and a side dish of steamed greens.

## Millet and Lentil Burgers

Serves 6.

*675 g/1½ lb millet, 2½ litres/4¼ pt water, 2 pinches sea salt, 170 g/6 oz whole brown or green lentils, 6 spring onions, cut into fine diagonal slices, 4 medium sized carrots, 2½ tablespoons barley miso, 1.5 cm/6 inch strip kombu, 3 teaspoons ginger juice (squeezed from freshly grated ginger), sesame oil*

Soak the kombu for 5 to 10 minutes and cut into very fine strips. Bring the water to a boil and add the kombu. Sort and wash the lentils and add to the water. Turn the heat to low and simmer for 30 minutes. Wash and dry roast the millet in a heavy-bottomed frying pan until it releases a nutty aroma. Add the millet to the lentils and simmer on a low flame for 40 minutes. Take off the heat.

Purée the miso with a little water and pour on the millet and lentils. Add the ginger juice and mix it in to the millet and lentils.

Wash and grate the carrots. Heat a frying pan and add 1 tablespoon of sesame oil. Sauté the grated carrot until it is sweet tasting — about 5 minutes. Add the sautéed carrot and cut spring onions to the millet mixture and mix well in.

Wet your hands and shape the millet mixture into flat rounds, squares, balls or croquette shapes. Heat 3 tablespoons of sesame oil in a large frying pan and fry these for 5 to 10 minutes on either side.

*Variations:* The millet and lentil burgers can be deep fried and served with a *Shoyu and ginger dip sauce* (see page 130).

*Serving suggestions:* Burgers are good served with a *Nishime* (see page 98) style vegetable dish and a light broccoli boiled salad with *Tofu spread* (see page 142) or *Miso relish* (see page 113).

## Millet and Chestnut Flan

Serves 6.

*450 g/1 lb millet, 1½ litres/2¾ pt water, 1 pinch sea salt, 2 tablespoons barley miso, 225 g/8 oz dried chestnuts, 1¼ litres/2¼ pt water, 9 medium carrots, 15 cm/6 inch kombu strip, 60 g/2 oz chopped parsley, 3 tablespoons sesame oil, 1 teaspoon dried basil, 4 tablespoons shoyu, 2 tablespoons white miso, 1 tablespoon kuzu*

Soak the chestnuts in the water for 4 hours or overnight.

Wash and prepare the millet as described on page 59. When the millet is cooked spoon it into a 30 cm/12 inch flan case and firmly press the millet to the sides and base of the flan case so that it resembles a pastry case. Bake the millet blind at 180°C/350°F/Gas Mark 4 for 25 minutes. Take the flan out of the oven and allow the millet to cool and harden slightly.

Wipe the kombu with a damp cloth to remove excess salt and place on the bottom of a pressure cooker. Add the chestnuts, chestnut soaking water, and 1 tablespoon shoyu, and pressure cook for 20 minutes. Take the chestnuts out of the pressure cooker and blend them either by hand in a suribachi or in a blender.

Cut the carrots into fine matchsticks. Heat a frying pan and add sesame oil. Add the carrots and sauté for 5 minutes, then add 1 tablespoon shoyu and sauté 2 minutes more. Layer the carrots inside the millet pastry case.

Place the puréed chestnuts back on the heat and add the basil. Blend the white miso with a little water and add this to the chestnuts. Blend the kuzu with a little cold water. Take the chestnut purée off the heat, add the kuzu and stir for 2 minutes while it thickens. Pour the chestnut purée over the carrots to fill the pastry case. Sprinkle the chopped parsley over liberally and serve either hot or cold.

*Serving suggestions:* Serve with a *Spring greens and sunflower salad* (see page 116) or coleslaw for a lunchtime meal.

### Deep-Fried Millet Balls

Serves 6.

*340 g/12 oz millet, 1 litre/2 pt water, 2 pinches of sea salt, 2 medium onions, 2 teapoons dried sage, 110 g/4 oz roasted and ground sesame seeds, 2 tablespoons white miso, sesame oil for deep-frying*

Cook the millet with the water and salt as described on page 59. Dice the onions finely and mix together with the cooked millet, sage and roasted and ground sesame seeds. Blend the white miso with a little cold water and stir this in.

Add sesame oil to a depth of 5 cm/2 inches in a saucepan and heat. To test whether the oil is ready, drop a piece of carrot into the oil — if the carrot rises to the surface immediately then the oil is ready for deep-frying.

Wet your hands and shape the millet mixture into small balls. Deep-fry 2 or 3 balls at a time until they are crisp and golden. Remove onto kitchen towel to drain.

*Serving suggestions:* Serve with cod steamed lightly in a steaming basket, corn and *Greens rolls* (see page 113).

## Millet and Almond Pasta Rolls

Serves 6.

*12 canelloni shells, 450 g/1 lb millet, $2\frac{3}{4}$ litres/5 pt water, 1 pinch sea salt, 1 tablespoon white miso, 1 carrot, grated finely, 2 teaspoons ginger juice (squeezed from freshly grated ginger), 170 g/6 oz almonds, sesame oil for deep-frying.*

Bring $1\frac{1}{2}$ litres/$2\frac{1}{2}$ pt water to a boil. Add the canelloni shells and cook for about 7 minutes. Take them out and rinse the shells well inside and out so that the starch doesn't make them too sticky to stuff with the millet and almonds. Set the canelloni shells aside for later.

Wash the millet in a sieve. Heat the remaining water, add a pinch of sea salt and the millet. Simmer on a very low heat for 35 to 40 minutes. Take the millet off the heat and mix in the white miso blended in a little water and the grated carrot.

Dry roast the almonds in a frying pan until they are golden brown and grind them to a powder in a coffee grinder. Add the almonds and ginger juice to the millet and mix well. Open out the canelloni shell gently by inserting a finger. Make some millet mixture into a fine sausage shape and push into the canelloni shell. Add more until the shell is completely full. Set the filled canelloni aside on a plate.

Pour sesame oil to a depth of 7.5 cm/3 inches in saucepan and heat. The oil is hot enough when a piece of vegetable dropped into it immediately rises to the surface. Deep fry 2 or 3 cannelloni at a time for 2 to 3 minutes until they are crisp and golden, then take them out with a slotted spoon onto kitchen towel to drain off excess oil. Allow the oil to re-heat between deep-frying more canelloni shells. Keep fried canelloni shells hot while the rest are frying, then serve.

*Serving suggestions:* Serve with a *Nishime* style dish of carrots and parsnips (see page 98) and a *Red radish and cucumber pressed salad* (see page 120).

### COUSCOUS

Couscous comes in two varieties; whole grain couscous which is usually organic and refined couscous which is white and readily available everywhere. White couscous works well in many recipes but lacks the more subtle and robust flavour of the whole grain couscous. Wholewheat couscous is also a more satisfying grain to eat, particularly with fish or white meat. White couscous tends to pick up on chemical additives readily. Generally try and choose a less refined couscous.

Couscous makes lovely cakes (see Desserts on page 146) and breads with the addition of seeds and nuts. Couscous is also good fried or made into a salad with peas and carrots.

**How to Cook Couscous**
Bring 570 ml/1 pt water per 225 g/8 oz couscous to a boil, add a pinch of salt per 225 g/8 oz couscous and then add the couscous. Simmer for 3 to 4 minutes with a lid on, then turn the heat off and allow the couscous to carry on cooking in its own heat for 10 to 15 minutes.

**Couscous Sauté**

Serves 6.

*675 g/1½ lb couscous, 1½ litres/2½ water, 3 medium onions, diced finely, 3 carrots, finely grated, 3 tablespoons sesame oil, 60 g/2 oz chopped parsley, 3 tablespoons white miso, 3 teaspoons ginger juice (squeezed from freshly grated ginger)*

Wash and cut the onions, carrots and parsley and put them in separate bowls. Heat a heavy-bottomed frying pan and add the oil. When the oil is hot, add the diced onion and sauté for 5 minutes. Add the grated carrot and sauté for 2 to 3 minutes. Blend the white miso in a little water and add to the onion and carrot. Turn the heat very low and cook for 1 to 2 minutes. Add the water, bring it to a simmer and add the couscous. Turn the heat very low and cover the pan with a good fitting lid. Leave the couscous on the heat for 3 to 4 minutes then take it off the heat and allow the couscous to cook in its own steam for 10 minutes. In the last 5 minutes add the parsley and ginger juice. When the couscous is cooked, fluff it with a pair of chopsticks or fork. Serve hot or cold.

*Serving suggestions:* This light grain dish makes a fine accompaniment to white fish and would go well with *Cod brightling* (see page 95) or the *Hake in thyme sauce* (see page 94). If serving with the hake and thyme sauce omit the ginger juice as too many different seasonings spoil a meal, the individual flavours getting lost.

## Couscous Loaf

Serves 4.

*340 g/12 oz couscous, 3 tablespoons sesame oil, 3 teaspoons mustard, 4 teaspoons barley miso, 60 g/2 oz finely chopped chives, 720 ml/1¼ pt water*

Heat the oil in a large frying pan. Add the couscous and sauté for 5 to 7 minutes, stirring continually until the couscous is golden in colour. This gives a lovely crunchy texture and rich flavour to the couscous. Bring the water to a boil in a separate saucepan and pour over the couscous. Place a lid over the couscous and turn the heat very low, allowing the couscous to simmer for 3 to 4 minutes.

Blend the miso in a little water, add with the mustard to the couscous and cook for 1 to 2 minutes. Remove the couscous from the heat and let it steam in its own heat for 10 minutes. Add the chives and mix them into the couscous.

Oil a round loaf tin or other bread tin. Press the couscous firmly into the tin so it is quite compacted and so slices well. Allow the loaf to cool for 1 to 2 hours before serving.

*Variations:* Roasted sunflower or pumpkin seeds or almonds or walnuts create a richer loaf. For a more warming recipe the couscous loaf can be baked in a moderate oven (180°C/350°F/ Gas Mark 4) for about 50 minutes.

*Serving suggestions:* This loaf is lovely cut in thin rounds and accompanied by vegetable dips like *Sunset dip* (see page 141) or *Pumpkin seed dressing* (see page 128). The loaf is also a good accompaniment at lunchtime to a thick soup or stew. A little raw salad completes the meal. Couscous loaf can be served with fish, particularly if the fish has a rich sauce such as *Whiting with tofu and onion sauce* (see page 92), *Hake in thyme sauce* (see page 94) or *Ling with almond and ginger sauce* (see page 93).

## Couscous Salad

Serves 4.

*225 g/8 oz couscous, 225 g/8 oz fresh peas, 570 g/1 pt water, 6 radishes, 3 tablespoons umeboshi vinegar*

Bring 570 ml/1 pt water to a boil and blanch the radishes whole. Rinse the radishes under cold water and cut them first into slices and then into very fine matchsticks. Marinate the matchsticks for 1 hour in 1 tablespoon of the umeboshi vinegar and 1 tablespoon water.

Pod and wash the peas. Steam the peas in ½ cm/¼ inch water for 5 minutes. Rinse in a sieve under cold water to heighten their colour and set aside until later.

Heat the water in a heavy-bottomed saucepan and add the couscous and 2 tablespoons of the umeboshi vinegar. Turn the heat very low, cover and cook for 3 to 4 minutes using a flame tamer if necessary. Take the couscous off the heat and allow it to cook in its own heat for 10 to 15 minutes. When the couscous is cooked but still warm, fluff the couscous with a pair of chopsticks or fork to separate the grains and make a lighter dish. Drain the radishes and mix with the peas into the couscous.

*Serving suggestions:* This salad could be served on a bed of lettuce or whole boiled spring greens or kale leaves. Garnish the salad with a few *Radish flowers* (see page 135). Couscous salad is an ideal grain to serve with fish.

## Couscous Rissoles

Serves 4

*675 g/1½ lb couscous, 1½ litres/2½ pt water, 110 g/4 oz sesame seeds, roasted and ground, 3 carrots, finely grated, 2 tablespoons white or barley miso or 1 tablespoon shoyu, 60 g/2 oz finely chopped parsley or chives, sesame oil*

Dry roast the sesame seeds in a frying pan until golden, then grind to a powder in a suribachi or coffee grinder. Bring the water to a boil, take 3 tablespoons and blend it with white miso to make a smooth paste. Return the miso and water to the saucepan and turn the heat to the lowest it will go. Add the couscous and cover with a lid. Leave the couscous on the heat for 3 to 4 minutes, then take the saucepan off the heat. Let the couscous cook in its own heat for 10 to 15 minutes, then mix in the parsley, grated carrot and sesame seeds.

Heat a frying pan and add 1 cm/½ inch sesame oil. Wet your hands lightly and make the couscous mixture into 8 to 12 rissoles. Fry gently on either side for 5 to 10 minutes depending on how crisp you like your rissoles. Longer frying needs a lower heat otherwise the outside of the rissole burns. Serve hot or cold.

*Serving suggestions:* Serve with a *Ginger shoyu dip sauce* (see page 130) or a ginger and shoyu kuzu sauce. Children love this recipe, it makes a good lunch or light meal. Serve together with a rich, long-cooked vegetable dish, such as a *Nishime* of carrots, cabbage and brussels sprouts (see page 98).

## BULGHUR WHEAT

Bulghur wheat is another fairly versatile grain and can be used for stuffing vegetables, baking in the oven or sautéeing with finely chopped vegetables. Bulghur wheat also makes lovely rissoles and steamed cakes.

### Bulghur Cabbage Rolls

Serves 6.

*450 g/1 lb bulghur wheat, 1 litre/2 pt water, 3 tablespoons sesame oil, 110 g/4 oz burdock, cut in thin diagonal slices (or onion half moons), 225 g/8 oz carrot, cut in thin diagonal slices, 2 tablespoons barley miso, 1 teaspoon prepared mustard, 6 cabbage leaves, 6 cocktail sticks*

Rinse the bulghur in a sieve and allow it to drain and swell for half an hour. Meanwhile cut the vegetables and heat the oil in a frying pan. Add the burdock or onion and sauté for 5 minutes. Add the carrots and sauté for 10 minutes, keeping the frying pan covered to stop the cooking juices evaporating.

Blend the barley miso with a small amount of water and add it to the vegetables, turn the heat low and simmer for 2 to 3 minutes. Add the mustard and cook for 1 minute. Add the bulghur and blend it in with the fried vegetables. Bring the water to a boil in a separate saucepan and pour into the bulghur. Cover the pan with a lid and cook on a low heat for 30 minutes, stirring occasionally.

Wash the cabbage leaves and remove the hard stem by cutting a V-shaped wedge from the base of each leaf. Place a rectangle of bulghur in the centre of each leaf, fold up the edges of the leaf over the top of the bulghur and roll the cabbage leaf up. Secure with a cocktail stick and place on an oiled baking tray. When all six have been prepared place the tray in an oven at 180°C/350°F/Gas Mark 4 for 30 to 40 minutes until just beginning to crisp.

*Serving suggestions:* Serve with *Peanut sauce* (see page 129) and a *Carrot, leek and cauliflower salad* (see page 117).

### Bulghur Stuffed Swedes

Serves 6.

*6 small round swedes or large white or golden ball turnips, 15 cm/6 inch strip of kombu, 450 g/1 lb bulghur wheat, 2 medium onions, diced, 1 tablespoon sesame oil, 2 teaspoons umeboshi paste, 60 g/2 oz finely chopped parsley, ½ packet dried mochi, 1½ tablespoons barley miso, 1 tablespoon mustard*

Wash the bulghur in a sieve and allow it to soak in 1 litre/2 pt water for 2 hours. Wipe the salt rime from a strip of kombu sea vegetable. Wash the swedes or turnips and cut a small slice from the base so that they stand up easily. Place the kombu then the swedes or turnips at the bottom of a large heavy-bottomed saucepan. Add 1 cm/½ inch of water and steam the swedes or turnips for 40 to 60 minutes. Remove the swedes or turnips and allow to cool slightly. Scoop out the centre of the swedes or turnips to make a hole 2.5 cm/1 inch to 3.5cm/½ inch wide.

Heat the oil in a large frying pan and add the diced onions. Sauté them on a medium heat for 10 minutes. Blend the umeboshi paste with 2 or 3 tablespoons of hot water, add to the onion and cook for 1 to 2 minutes more. Add the bulghur and its soaking water and cover with a lid. Turn the heat very low and cook for 30 minutes. Remove the bulghur from the heat and allow it to cool. Stuff the turnips or swedes with the bulghur wheat.

Heat 2.5 cm/1 inch of water in a cast iron or heavy-bottomed frying pan. Grate or finely slice the dried mochi and simmer for 5 minutes until the mochi softens and thickens to make a sauce. Blend the miso in 2 tablespoons of water and add to the mustard. Add the miso and mustard to the mochi and simmer for 2 minutes more. Add the finely chopped parsley and simmer for 1 minute by which time the mochi should be a stiff sauce.

Preheat the oven to 180°C/350°F/Gas Mark 4. Place the turnips or swedes on a baking tray and spoon the mochi over the top and so it runs as a glaze down the sides. Put the turnips or swedes in the oven for 20 to 25 minutes until the mochi is crispy and golden. Serve hot. This makes a delicious and sustaining grain side dish served with a little rice or noodles.

*Variations:* Heat the juice of half a lemon and pour a little over each turnip or swede. You can also make this recipe into turnip or swede cups if you prefer by scooping out the middle of the turnips or swedes and filling the cup with bulghur and mochi.

*Serving suggestions:* Serve with *Rice and black soya beans* (see *Rice, sweet rice and chestnut variations* page 56) and a salad of broccoli florets and carrot matchsticks with *Sesame rice vinegar and umeboshi dressing* (see page 129). A few *Onion miso quick pickles* (see page 133) would be delicious here.

### Bulghur Mousse

Serves 6.

*675 g/1½ lb bulghur wheat, 2 litres/3½ pt water, 110 g/4 oz diced onion, 2 tablespoons sesame oil, 110 g/4 oz finely grated carrot, 1½ tablespoons mustard, 1 lemon rind, grated, 7 teaspoons shoyu, 60 g/2 oz parsley or spring onion, finely chopped, 1 tablespoon white miso*

Rinse the bulghur wheat in a sieve, drain it, and leave to swell for half an hour. Bring the water to a boil and add the bulghur and shoyu. Turn the heat very low and simmer the bulghur gently for 40 minutes. Turn off the heat and let the bulghur sit covered for 10 minutes.

Meanwhile heat the oil in a large frying pan. Add the diced onion and sauté on a medium heat until it becomes transparent. Add the grated carrot and sauté for about 5 minutes until it smells really sweet. Add the bulghur wheat and sauté a further 2 minutes. Mix the white miso, mustard and a little water to a paste, mix in with the bulghur, and sauté for 3 minutes. Turn the heat off and add the parsley or spring onions. Press the bulghur into individual ramekins and chill for 2 hours before serving.

*Serving suggestions:* Bulghur mousse goes really well with fish such as whole grilled trout with almonds and ginger and a raw side salad of lettuce and cucumber, onion rings and *Pumpkin seed spread* (see page 128).

## NOODLES

Noodles are very quick to cook and can be used to make very rich dishes. They are very popular with children who love a bowl full of different shaped noodles. Adults seem to love them too as they are easily digestible and make a light snack, salad or supper. Noodles can be used fried, as salads and in sushi.

There are many different kinds of noodles. My preference is for Udon noodles which are long and white, flavourful and easy to digest. I also use wholewheat pasta in different dishes, some days one shape, another day a different shape. Children love to choose what shape to buy and eat for lunch. I also use buckwheat noodles which are very vitalizing.

### Noodle, Carrot Flower and Broccoli Floret Salad

Serves 6.

*450 g/1 lb twisted wholewheat noodles or wholewheat pasta wheels, 1 pinch of sea salt, 8 large carrots cut into carrot flowers (see page 43), 450 g/1 lb broccoli cut into medium sized florets, 170 g/6 oz sesame seeds, 290 ml/½ pt rice vinegar, 2½ tablespoons shoyu, 15 cm/6 inch strip of kombu*

Bring to a boil two saucepans each containing about 860 ml/1½ pt water. Add a pinch of salt to one saucepan and the pasta. Simmer for 12 to 15 minutes. When it has finished cooking place the pasta in a sieve and rinse under cold water.

To the other saucepan add the kombu and let it simmer in the water for 3 to 4 minutes. Remove the kombu and set it aside for use in another dish. Add the carrot flowers and boil them for 1 minute. Take the carrots out with a slotted spoon and run them gently under cold water in a sieve. This stops the carrots cooking further, brightens the orange colour, brings out the flavour and gives a lovely cool, crisp texture to the carrots. Then cook the broccoli florets for 2 to 3 minutes and run them under cold water as with the carrots. Drain the broccoli and carrots and mix them with the noodles in a large wooden or ceramic serving bowl.

Wash the sesame seeds in a sieve and dry roast them in a heavy-bottomed frying pan on a high flame, stirring continuously. When the seeds powder easily when rubbed between your thumb and third finger, remove the seeds and grind them to a powder in a coffee grinder. Blend the sesame seeds, shoyu and rice vinegar with enough water to make a smooth sauce consistency and pour over the salad.

*Variations:* Fry very small squares of tofu seasoned with miso and mix with the salad. Small cubes of seitan could be used similarly.

*Serving suggestions:* For a light lunch serve as it is with *Deep fried tempeh* (see page 80) and sauerkraut.

### Leek and Umeboshi Noodle Salad

Serves 6.

*450 g/1 lb udon noodles or wholewheat spaghetti, 3 medium sized leeks, 3 umeboshi plums, 290 ml/½ pt water to mix*

Bring about 1¾ litres/3 pt water to a boil and add the noodles. Simmer gently for 10 to 12 minutes. Noodles are always more delicious and digestible if they are cooked on a low heat. Place them in a sieve and run them gently under cold water. Drain off excess liquid and place the noodles in a serving bowl.

Bring 570 ml/1 pt water to a boil. Wash and cut the leeks finely on the diagonal. When the water has come to a boil add the white half of the leeks. After one minute add the green half of the leeks and cook one minute more. Rinse the leeks in a sieve under gently running water, then leave to drain for a few minutes while you make up the umeboshi dressing.

Mash the umeboshi plums in a small bowl and remove the stones. Place the flesh of the plums in a small jar with the cup of water. Screw the lid on tightly and shake the jar vigorously until the water changes colour to a bright reddy-orange.

Mix the drained leeks with the Udon noodles and pour the umeboshi dressing over.

*Variations:* There are many variations to this dish. Grated carrot and mustard cress can be added or roasted sunflower or pumpkin seeds. Walnuts or almonds can be roasted, chopped and mixed in.

*Serving suggestions:* Serve with fish or on its own as a summer salad alongside *Millet and lentil burgers* (see page 60).

## Noodle Sushi

Serves 6.

*450 g/1 lb udon noodles or buckwheat noodles, 2 bunches watercress, 3 carrots, cut into matchsticks, 6 sheets of nori, 3 tablespoons tahini, 2 tablespoons umeboshi paste (or 3 umeboshi plums)*

Bring 1¾ litres/3 pt water to a boil, add the noodles and simmer on a low heat for 10 to 12 minutes. Then rinse in a sieve under a tap and drain.

Wash the watercress, blanch if desired or leave raw and place it on a plate to drain. Wash the carrots and cut into matchsticks. Mix the tahini and umeboshi paste together in a suribachi or bowl.

Take the 6 sheets of nori and toast them one by one over a low gas flame. Hold each sheet of nori 10 cm/4 inches above the flame and move it to and fro until the nori changes colour from brown to green. If you use electricity, hold very close to a ring turned up high. Lay one sheet of nori on a bamboo sushi mat and place ⅙th of the noodles across the nori in parallel lines. Make a line of carrot matchsticks and watercress in the middle of the noodles. Spread some of the tahini sauce over the vegetables and noodles.

Roll the nori up in the mat, pulling back the edge of the mat so that it doesn't get caught up in the roll. As you roll, press the nori and noodles firmly together to make a compact roll, or the sushi will tend to fall to pieces. When the nori is completely rolled up, wrap the sushi mat around it and squeeze gently but firmly to make the roll stick together. Unwrap the roll and cut into 6 or 7 sushi. This is a difficult process, but with practice you will be making fine sushi. Repeat with the remaining ingredients.

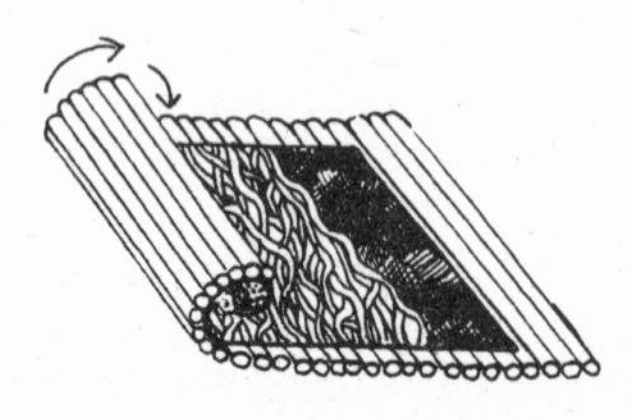

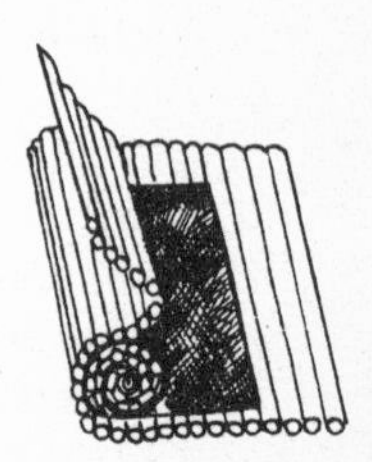

*Variations:* Noodle sushi can be filled with many bought spreads such as lentil spread or tofu spread. Other possibilities are mustard cress, spring onions, fried tofu fingers that have been marinated in umeboshi vinegar and pickled greens. Sour and salty tastes seem to work best inside sushi. Mustard and miso with carrot matchsticks is a nice combination. Rice sushi can be made in the same way by spreading boiled or pressure cooked rice out on the nori instead of the noodles.

*Serving suggestions:* Sushi really make a meal in themselves. They are ideal for a picnic or light lunch for children. They are also a great party food.

## Scrambled Tofu With Pasta Shells

Serves 4.

*450 g/1 lb pasta shells, 225 g/8 oz squash cut in small cubes (alternatively use diced carrots), 2 × 340 g/12 oz blocks tofu, 6 spring onions (or chives) chopped finely, 3 tablespoons barley miso, 2 tablespoons sesame oil*

Bring 1 litre/2 pt water to a boil and add the pasta shells. Turn the heat very low, cover the pot and cook for 10 to 15 minutes.

While the pasta is cooking, heat 1 tablespoon of the oil in a heavy-bottomed frying pan. Add the squash cubes and fry them for 10 minutes. Add 150 ml/¼ pt of water and cook the squash 5 minutes longer. Blend the squash to a sauce in a blender with a ½ tablespoon of the miso and 4 of the chopped spring onions.

Wash the frying pan and heat the other tablespoon of sesame oil. Crumble the tofu between your fingers into a bowl and add to the hot oil. Sauté for 3 minutes. Blend the remaining 2 tablespoons of miso with 2 tablespoons water and pour it over the tofu. Cook the tofu and miso for 2 minutes, turn off the heat and add the remaining chopped spring onion.

Mix the pasta shells, squash purée and tofu mixture together and serve.

## Tofu Lasagne

Serves 6.

*10 sheets wholewheat lasagne pasta, 1 litre/2 pt water, 3 leeks, cut diagonally, 110 g/4 oz mushrooms, sliced, 5 medium carrots, grated, 1 tablespoon sesame oil, 1 teaspoon shoyu, 2 × 340 g/12 oz blocks firm tofu, 110 g/4 oz sesame seeds, 1 tablespoon miso*

Bring the water to a boil and add the lasagne sheets one at a time. Cook for 15 minutes, then briefly rinse each sheet under running water and set aside.

Heat the oil in a large frying pan and sauté the grated carrot on a medium heat for 5 minutes. Add the leeks and sauté for 3 minutes. Add the mushrooms and shoyu, sauté a further 5 minutes and turn off.

Sort and wash the sesame seeds and roast on a medium heat stirring constantly. The seeds are done when they can be easily crushed between the thumb and third finger. Grind the seeds in a suribachi or coffee grinder. Purée the tofu and miso in a suribachi or blender and stir in half the sesame seeds.

Spread 2½ sheets of pasta on the bottom of an ovenproof glass dish then spread a third of the vegetables on top. Add another layer of pasta, then vegetables, and so on ending with a layer of pasta. Spread the tofu and miso mixture over the top. Cook in a pre-heated oven at 190°C/350°F/Gas Mark 5 for 15 to 20 minutes. Garnish with the remaining sesame seeds and serve.

*Variations:* Instead of tofu, make a lentil, carrot and garlic purée with spring onions.

*Serving suggestions:* Tofu lasagne makes a well-balanced meal when combined with a lighter pressed or boiled salad, as it contains a grain, vegetables, and tofu as a rich source of protein.

## Sourdough Pancakes

Serves 6.

*225 g/8 oz 81 per cent wholemeal or 70 per cent strong white flour, 1 pinch of sea salt, sesame oil*

Mix the flour with enough water to make a thin batter consistency. Cover with a cloth and leave in a warm place to sour for 2 to 4 days. It should develop a sour smell. If it becomes putrid or mouldy it has been left too long. After souring add a pinch of salt (or green nori flakes for very young children).

Lightly brush a frying pan with the oil and heat on a medium to high heat. When the oil is hot enough a drop of batter will instantly sizzle. Pour in the batter to thinly cover the bottom of the pan. Cook for 2 to 3 minutes until the underside of the pancake lightly browns, then turn over and cook the other side for about a minute.

*Pancake fillings:* Pancakes are lovely with sweet or savoury fillings. Here are a few for you to try:

- Sweet and sour sauté, made by sautéing 4 grated carrots, 225 g/8 oz white cabbage cut in thin slithers, and 1 bunch of

watercress. Add shoyu, rice or cider vinegar and mirin or barley malt for seasoning.
- Any cooked beans such as lentils and onions.
- Hot barley malt or rice syrup with lemon juice.

*Variations:* Make broccoli pancakes by first boiling 110 g/4 oz broccoli for 10 minutes, then half a bunch of watercress for 4 minutes. Drain well then dry roast in a frying pan for 1 to 2 minutes to dry thoroughly. Cut the broccoli and watercress finely and purée in a suribachi or blender. Mix the puréed greens with the pancake mixture and make pancakes as above. If necessary add a little kuzu or arrowroot powder to the pancake mixture to thicken it. Broccoli pancakes are delicious with *Tofu spread* (see page 142) rolled inside them.

# 9. BEANS, FISH AND OTHER HIGH-PROTEIN FOODS

Fish is an excellent source of protein and there are many good vegetable and grain sources of protein too. *Seitan* is made from wheat protein. It is very strengthening and when deep-fried tastes somewhat like chicken. *Tempeh* is a fermented soya bean cheese and is now readily available from many shops around the country. *Mochi* is made by pounding sweet rice. It is sweet but is used in both savoury dishes and desserts. *Tofu* is a soya bean curd. It can be bought ready-made in many shops and is lighter and more easily digestible than tempeh. It is excellent for making creamy sauces and dressings.

There are also many types of beans to use on a regular basis. The best varieties to use most often are aduki beans, chick peas, green or brown lentils and black soya beans, because they are the most yang of the beans and so more vitalizing for the body.

## SEITAN

### How to Make Seitan

Serves 6.

*1¼ kg/3 lb unbleached strong white flour or 81 per cent wholewheat flour, 15 cm/6 inch strip of kombu, 6 tablespoons shoyu, 110 g/4 oz fresh ginger root, cut into thick slices*

It is very important to use fresh flour, as the protein decays in old flour, making it impossible to make seitan from it. Mix water with the flour to make a firm dough and knead it for 4 or 5 minutes. Place it in a bowl with cold water to cover and allow it to sit for at least 30 minutes.

Knead the dough in a bowl of cold water until the water becomes thick and white. Pour the water away (or keep this starch for thickening sauces instead of using arrowroot or kuzu). Fill the bowl with warm water, knead again, and pour of the starchy water. Repeat this process, alternating cold and hot water, until all the starch has been washed out, leaving the water clear. You will then have a stretchy ball of wheat protein left.

Bring about 1¾ litres/3 pt water to a boil and add the kombu, shoyu and ginger slices. Break the wheat protein into small balls, drop into the water and simmer for 30 minutes to 1 hour. Longer cooking gives a more robust flavour to the seitan. Store the seitan in a refrigerator and use over the next 3 or 4 days.

**Sweet 'n' Sour Seitan**

Serves 6.

*560 g/1½ lb cooked seitan, cut in cubes, 1 tablespoon shoyu, 8 large onions, cut into thin half-moons, 1½ bunches of watercress, chopped, 6 tablespoons sesame oil, 290 ml/½ pt rice vinegar, 2 tablespoons umeboshi paste*

Heat 2 tablespoons of the oil in a large frying pan on a medium heat. Add the seitan cubes and sauté until golden. Add the shoyu and cook 2 minutes more. Place the seitan in a bowl for use later.

Wash the frying pan and replace it on the heat. Add the remaining 4 tablespoons of sesame oil and when the oil is hot but not smoking, add the onions. Sauté on a medium heat for about 25 minutes until very soft and sweet. Add a little water if necessary to prevent the onions burning.

Add the seitan cubes to the onions in the frying pan. Blend the rice vinegar and umeboshi paste together in a suribachi or cup and add to the pan. Sauté very gently for 4 to 5 minutes. Wash and cut the watercress stalks and leaves into 1 cm/½ inch pieces and add to the pan. Sauté briefly and serve hot.

*Serving suggestions:* Serve with *Rice and barley* (see page 58), together with steamed cabbage or kale and *Brine pickles* (see page 132).

### Pasta el Fagioli

Serves 6.

*450 g/1 lb cooked seitan, cut into cubes, 450 g/1 lb cooked wholewheat pasta shells or udon noodles, 4 onions, diced, 6 carrots, cut into matchsticks, 6 tablespoons sesame oil, 450 g/ 1 lb cooked aduki beans, 4 tablespoons shoyu, 1 teaspoon dried oregano or basil, 6 cloves garlic, chopped finely*

Heat the oil in a large frying pan and add the finely chopped garlic. Sauté on a medium heat for 5 minutes but do not burn it. Add the diced onion and sauté until the onion is transparent. Add the carrot matchsticks and sauté for 10 to 15 minutes. Add the seitan cubes and shoyu and sauté for 2 to 3 minutes before adding the aduki beans. Cook with the beans for 10 minutes and mix in the cooked pasta shells and oregano. Sauté for 2 to 3 minutes more and then serve hot.

*Serving suggestions*: Serve with a raw salad with oil and vinegar dressing.

### Seitan Stroganoff

Serves 6.

*3 tablespoons sesame oil, 560 g/1¼ lb cooked seitan, cut into thin slices, 450 g/1 lb carrot matchsticks, 170 g/6 oz firm tofu, 2 teaspoons miso, 425 ml/¾ pt vegetable stock, 1 tablespoon grated ginger, 3 tablespoons mirin or 1½ tablespoons rice vinegar, 1 bunch of watercress, spring onions or parsley, chopped finely to garnish*

Heat 2 tablespoons of the sesame oil in a large frying pan. Add the slices of seitan and sauté for about 5 minutes until golden. Blend 1 teaspoon of the miso in a little water, add to the seitan and sauté 1 to 2 minutes longer. Set aside the seitan until later.

Rinse the frying pan and place on a medium heat. Add the remaining 4 tablespoons of oil and when it is hot add the carrot matchsticks. Sauté over a low heat for about fifteen minutes.

Meanwhile steam the block of tofu in ½ cm/¼ inch of water for 10 minutes, then purée it together with the grated ginger and miso in a blender. Add vegetable water as necessary to make a runny sauce.

Add the mirin to the carrot and sauté for 1 minute, then add the tofu sauce. Cook the tofu sauce with the carrot until it is rich and creamy. Add the fried seitan and add more seasoning if necessary. Serve and garnish with the spring onions, watercress or parsley.

*Serving suggestions*: Serve hot with rice and sunflower seeds, steamed onions, and a *Carrot, broccoli and red radish boiled salad* (see page 115).

## Deep-Fried Stuffed Seitan

Serves 6.

*675 g/1½ lb unbleached strong white flour, 4 carrots, 2 spring onions, 15 cm/6 inch strip of kombu, 60 g/2 oz ginger, 4 tablespoons shoyu, 2 tablespoons miso, sesame or safflower oil for deep-frying*

Cut the carrots into large matchsticks and spread a thin layer of the miso over them. Allow the carrot to sit and pickle in the miso for 3 hours.

Use the flour to make a dough and wash it, as described in *How to make seitan* on page 76. Wash and slice the spring onions into 2.5 cm/1 inch lengths. Put 1½ litres/2½ pt water on to boil. Break the wheat protein (seitan) into lumps the size of a small apple. Stretch one piece of wheat protein out to make a flat sheet and place 2 pieces of carrot and 2 or 3 pieces of spring onion in the centre. Roll the wheat protein around the carrot and spring onion and hold for a minute or until it has firmly joined to make a log-shape. Repeat until there is at least one stuffed seitan roll per person. If the seitan is stretched too thin it puffs up while cooking.

To the boiling water add the kombu, shoyu and the ginger cut into small knobs. Place the seitan rolls gently in the water so that they don't stick together. After the first few minutes of cooking they won't stick together anyway. Simmer the seitan for at least 30 minutes and not longer than an hour.

Remove the seitan and drain it for a few minutes on kitchen towel. Pour the oil to a depth of 7.5 cm/3 inches in a pan and heat. When a small piece of vegetable dropped into the oil immediately rises bubbling to the surface, the oil is hot enough. Deep-fry each seitan roll for about 3 minutes and serve with a *Ginger shoyu dip sauce* (see page 130) or *Mustard shoyu dip sauce* (see page 130).

*Variations:* Stuff the seitan with onion, miso and mustard.

*Serving suggestions:* Serve with *Rice and oats* (see page 55), steamed onions and broccoli and *Carrot and cucumber salad* (see page 120).

## TEMPEH

The traditional way of cooking tempeh to enhance its flavour and digestibility is to boil it with a 15 cm/6 inch strip of kombu and a tablespoon of shoyu or miso per 225 g/8 oz block. Bring the tempeh to a boil on a high flame, turn the heat to medium and cook the tempeh for at least 35 minutes. Once the tempeh has been cooked in this way it can be added to soups and stews, casseroles and sea vegetable dishes. It can also be fried with ginger and shoyu, mirin and shoyu or lemon juice and shoyu.

### Deep-fried Tempeh

Serves 6.

*1½ × 225 g/8 oz block tempeh, 290 ml/½ pt sesame or sunflower oil for deep-frying, 1½ tablespoon ginger juice (squeezed from freshly grated ginger), 2 tablespoons shoyu, 3 tablespoons water*

Cook the tempeh as described above, then cut the blocks of tempeh so that they are half their original thickness. Then cut into fingers, squares or triangles. Heat the oil in a pan until a small piece of vegetable dropped into it quickly rises sizzling to the surface. Cook a few pieces of tempeh together for 2 to 3 minutes or until crisp and golden. Remove onto kitchen paper to drain. Add more pieces of tempeh, ensuring that the oil stays hot enough all the time.

Mix the ginger juice, shoyu and water and serve in an attractive bowl, as a sauce to dip the fried tempeh in.

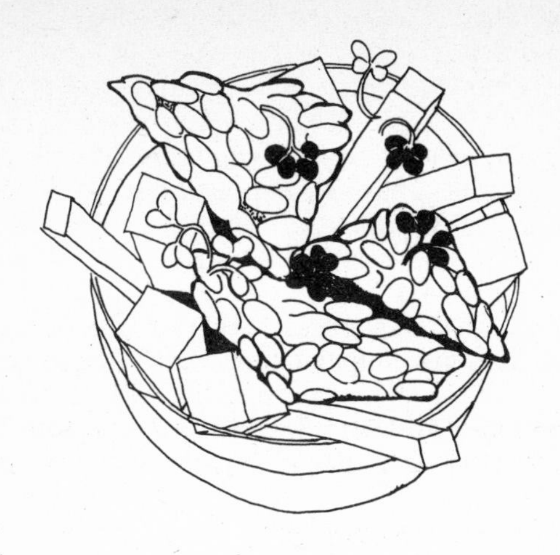

*Serving suggestions:* Fingers or triangles can be arranged decoratively on a serving platter with the dipping bowl in the centre. They can be served with *Rice and barley* (see page 58) and a *Red radish and cucumber pressed salad* (see page 120).

## Tempeh with Onions, Kombu and Umeboshi

Serves 6.

*1½ × 225 g/8 oz blocks of tempeh, 2 umeboshi plums, 15 cm/ 6 inch strip of kombu, 6 medium onions, 1½ tablespoons sauerkraut, 425 ml/¾ pt water*

Wipe the excess salt off the kombu with a damp cloth and soak the kombu in enough water to cover for one hour. This makes the kombu softer. Cut the kombu into fine strips and layer it on the bottom of a heavy-based saucepan. Cut the onions into half moons (see page 42) and place them on top of the kombu. Place the umeboshi in the centre of the onion. Cut the tempeh into cubes of about 1 cm/½ inch square and spread over the onions. Add the kombu soaking water and enough additional water to make a total of about 425 ml/¾ pt water and steam the dish on a medium heat for 40 minutes. Add a little more water to prevent burning if necessary. Spread the sauerkraut gently over the tempeh. Cook 5 minutes more and serve this dish hot. This dish has a lovely sweet and salty flavour.

*Serving suggestions:* Serve for lunch with *Noodle Sushi* (see page 72) or for supper with rice, *Nishime* carrots (see page 98) and kale boiled salad.

## Arame, Tempeh, Carrot and Onion

Serves 6.

*60 g/2 oz of arame sea vegetable, 4 medium carrots, cut into large matchsticks, 3 medium sized onions, cut in thick half moons (see page 42), 1 × 225 g/8 oz tempeh, cut into cubes, 1 bunch of watercress, 1½ tablespoon shoyu*

Place the arame in a sieve and rinse it under a cold tap. Put the arame in the bottom of a saucepan and layer first the carrots, then the onion, then the tempeh on top. Add 290 ml/½ pt water and 1 tablespoon of the shoyu and simmer the dish for about 1 hour and 10 minutes. Add more water as it becomes necessary to prevent burning. Do not add too much water at one time as it devitalizes the dish and it is not so flavoursome. At the end of cooking remove the lid and cook away nearly all the remaining liquid.

Cut the watercress into 2.5 cm/1 inch lengths and add to the pan. Steam the watercress for 2 to 3 minutes then serve this dish hot.

*Serving suggestions:* Have for lunch with a noodle salad or *Couscous rissoles* (see page 66) and boiled cabbage.

### MOCHI

Mochi is made from sweet rice, a more glutinous form of rice from the Orient which is higher in protein than ordinary rice. It is very good for anyone in a devitalized condition and for pregnant and nursing women.

Because of its texture, mochi can be used as a substitute for cheese in some dishes — place a layer of mochi and miso over baked onion, squash or carrots and grill it or bake it for 5 to 10 minutes.

Dried mochi can be bought from certain natural food shops, sealed in cellophane so that it keeps indefinitely. Once opened keep dried mochi covered in the fridge.

## Mochi Balls

Serves 6.

*450 g/1 lb sweet rice, 570 ml/1 pt water, 2 pinches of sea salt,225 g/8 oz sesame seeds, 110 g/4 oz green nori flakes*

Wash the rice and place it in a pressure cooker. Add the water and sea salt. Bring up to pressure and turn the heat low. For best results, use a flame tamer which prevents the sweet rice scorching on the bottom. Pressure cook for 20 minutes then take it off the heat and allow the pressure to come down naturally.

When the rice has cooled a little, pound it with the end of a suribachi handle or rolling pin until it becomes a glutinous cream. To make real mochi takes about an hour's pounding, so *ohagi* is often made instead — this is half pounded mochi. If possible let the mochi sit for a few hours to stiffen.

Wash and dry roast the sesame seeds over a medium heat, stirring continuously for about 5 minutes. The seeds should be lightly golden but not brown. Grind the seeds in a coffee grinder or suribachi and mix them with the green nori flakes. Place the seeds and nori flakes in a bowl.

Wet your hands under running water and shape the mochi into little balls. Roll the balls in the toasted sesame seeds and green nori flakes and place decoratively on a plate. A carrot flower (see page 43) can be placed on each mochi ball.

### Mochi Stuffed Turnip Cups

Serves 6.

*450 g/1 lb sweet rice, made into mochi as described in Mochi Balls on page 82, 6 large turnips, 6 onions diced finely, 2 leeks, 3 tablespoons white miso, 3 teaspoons mustard, chopped spring onions to garnish*

Steam the turnips for 10 minutes using a steaming basket or 1 cm/½ inch water in a pan. Scoop out the centre of the turnips to make a hole 2.5 to 5 cm/1 to 2 inches wide and deep.

Heat a 1 cm/½ inch water in a heavy-bottomed frying pan and add the diced onions. Sauté the onions for 15 to 20 minutes until they are very soft and sweet. Add more water to keep the bottom of the pan covered when necessary. Cut the leeks into thin rings and sauté them with the onion for 2 minutes. Blend 1 tablespoon of white miso in 1 tablespoon of water, add to the pan and cook 1 minute more. Remove from the heat and fill the turnip cups with the onion and leek so that they are very full.

Blend the remaining 2 tablespoons of miso in a little water and mix with the mustard and mochi. Spread a layer of mochi over each turnip cup. Place the cups under the grill for 5 to 10 minutes until the mochi is puffed and golden. Garnish with spring onions.

*Serving suggestion:* Serve the turnip cups for lunch with a *Noodle, carrot flower and broccoli salad* (see page 70) and *Greens rolls* (see page 113).

## BEANS

### Chick pea el Rondo

Serves 6.

*450 g/1 lb chick peas, 2 litres/3½ pt water, 15 cm/6 inch strip of kombu, 3 tablespoons shoyu, 4 tablespoons tahini, 5 onions, 8 carrots, 5 spring onions, parsley to garnish*

Pick any stones out of the chick peas, wash, and soak overnight. Discard the soaking water. Wipe the salt rime from the kombu with a damp cloth and place in the bottom of a pressure cooker. Place the chick peas on top of the kombu and add the water. Pressure cook the chick peas for 30 minutes, then remove from the heat and allow the pressure to come down.

Cut the onions into quarters. Bring the chick peas back to a boil, add the onions and simmer gently for approximately 10 minutes with the lid off so that the more pungent elements of the onion are lost. Cut the carrots into 2.5 cm/1 inch chunks and add to the pan with the shoyu. Simmer gently for 50 minutes to 1 hour. Blend the tahini with 2 to 3 tablespoons of water, pour over the chick peas, and cook without a lid until all the liquid has been absorbed. Add the spring onions and remove the saucepan from the heat.

Transfer half the chick peas to a suribachi and blend them to a paste. Mix this with the rest of the chick peas. Wet your hands lightly and roll the chick peas into balls, log shapes or patties and garnish with parsley. Serve chilled.

*Serving suggestions:* Serve with rice garnished with roasted black sesame seeds and green nori flakes and *Carrot, broccoli and red radish boiled salad* (see page 115). Alternatively serve with *Noodle sushi* (see page 72) and *Peanut sauce* (see page 129).

### Aduki Beans, Kombu and Squash

Serves 6.

*450 g/1 lb aduki beans, 225 g/8 oz cubed pumpkin or squash — if pumpkin isn't available use carrots, onions or parsnips, 2 × 15 cm/6 inch strips of kombu, 3 tablespoons shoyu, parsley to garnish*

Pick any stones out of the aduki beans, then wash in a sieve and drain. It is better not to soak the aduki beans in this recipe, as then they are not so strengthening.

Wipe the excess salt from the kombu with a damp cloth and place in the bottom of a heavy-bottomed saucepan. Layer the aduki beans on top and add enough water to cover them. Bring to a boil and simmer on a high heat for 1 hour and 20 minutes. Top up the water level when necessary to keep the beans covered by pouring water down the side of the saucepan. This is known as the *shocking method* of cooking beans, where the sudden influx of cold water makes the beans contract, taking the heat into the centre of the beans so that they cook more quickly.

Add the pumpkin and shoyu and cook for 50 minutes longer. Salt or salty seasonings are added near the end of cooking, rather than at the beginning when they would make the beans more contracted and lengthen their cooking time. Place the beans in a serving dish and garnish with the chopped parsley. The pumpkin or carrot will become very soft and sweet. This makes a marvellously warming dish, very good for the kidneys and general vitality.

### Lentil Pâté

Serves 6.

*450 g/1 lb brown, green or Puy speckled lentils, 1¼ litres/2¼ pt water, 2 × 15 cm/6 inch strips of kombu, 2 teaspoons shoyu, 6 spring onions, 6 carrots, 1½ tablespoons umeboshi vinegar, 1½ tablespoons white miso or 1 tablespoon barley miso, 3 sprigs of chives, finely chopped, 3 tablespoons sesame oil*

Wash the lentils in a sieve and sort through for stones. Wipe the salt rime from the kombu with a damp cloth and place in the bottom of a heavy-bottomed saucepan. Add the lentils, cover with the water and bring to a boil. Turn the heat down, cover and simmer very gently for 50 minutes.

While the lentils are cooking, wash and grate the carrots and cut the spring onions finely on the diagonal. Heat a heavy-bottomed frying pan and add the sesame oil. When the oil is hot, add the grated carrot and sauté for about 5 minutes until the carrot is soft and sweet. Add the spring onion and sauté a further 3 minutes.

Add the sautéed carrot, spring onions and shoyu to the lentils and simmer for 20 minutes more. The lentils should then be dry. If not, simmer without a lid until all the water has cooked away. Take the lentils off the heat and add the umeboshi vinegar, miso and half the chopped chives. Blend the ingredients together and press into a stainless steel bread tin or a pyrex loaf dish. Make sure you compact the lentils firmly into the mould. Allow the pâté to cool and set for at least 2 hours — refrigerate if necessary. Turn the pâté out and garnish it with the rest of the chives.

*Serving suggestion:* Serve with pitta bread or crackers and thin slices of cucumber or sauerkraut. This pâté is nice served in individual ramekins to go with *Rice salad* (see pages 57 and 58) or *Rice and wheat* (see page 55).

**Black Bean and Carrot Medley**

Serves 6.

*15 cm/6 inch strip of kombu, 450 g/1 lb black beans, 2¾ litres/5 pt water, 9 large carrots, cut in chunks, 6 medium onions, cut in half moons (see page 42), 2 tablespoons shoyu, 60 g/2 oz finely chopped parsley*

Wash the beans quickly in a sieve and soak in water to cover. Add a small pinch of salt to the soaking water to prevent the skins falling off and soak the beans overnight.

Discard the bean soaking water. Wipe the salt rime from the kombu and place in the bottom of a pressure cooker. Place the beans on top and add 1¾ litres/3 pt water. Pressure cook the beans for 15 minutes.

Transfer the kombu, beans and cooking water to a heavy-bottomed saucepan. Add the onions to the beans and simmer gently for 5 minutes. Add the carrots to the beans with the shoyu. Cook the beans and vegetables gently for 1 hour. Add more of the water as necessary to keep the beans covered. Add the parsley in the last 10 minutes or cooking. Remove the lid and cook away any remaining liquid. To achieve this without burning you can use a flame tamer.

*Serving suggestions:* Serve with rice garnished with *Sesame shiso leaf condiment* (see page 138) and white cabbage and parsley boiled salad (see page 115 on how to prepare boiled salads).

### Aduki and Chestnut Balls

Serves 6.

*450 g/1 lb aduki beans, 225 g/8 oz dried chestnuts, 1½ tablespoons shoyu, grated rind of 1 lemon or tangerine, 2 × 15 cm/6 inch strips of kombu, 170 g/6 oz sunflower seeds*

Soak the chestnuts overnight in enough water to cover. Pick any stones out of the aduki beans and wash in a sieve. Wipe the excess salt from the kombu with a damp cloth and place in the bottom of a saucepan. Add the soaked chestnuts, chestnut soaking water and aduki beans with enough water to cover and simmer for 1 hour 20 minutes. Add more water when necessary to keep the beans and chestnuts covered.

Add the shoyu and cook for another 50 minutes. Add more water if necessary, but at the end let all the water cook away so that the aduki and chestnut mixture is quite dry. A flame tamer can be used to prevent burning.

Remove the aduki and chestnut mixture from the heat and purée it in a suribachi or blender. Mix in the grated lemon rind and roll into balls. Roast the sunflower seeds until golden and chop them up with a knife. Roll the balls in the chopped seeds and serve.

### Red Kidney Beans, Kombu and Carrots

Serves 6.

*450 g/1 lb red kidney beans, 1¾ litres/3 pt water, 4 onions, 10 carrots, 2 × 15 cm/6 inch strips of kombu, 2 tablespoons shoyu, 60 g/2 oz chopped parsley*

Wash the beans and soak overnight.

Discard the bean soaking water and pressure cook them with the kombu and water for 20 minutes. Remove the beans from the heat and allow the pressure to come down. Cut the onions into half moons (see page 42), add to the beans and simmer for 20 minutes. Then cut the carrots into chunks and place them on top of the onions. Add the shoyu. Place the lid of the pressure cooker on lightly so that the food steams and cook the beans and vegetables gently for 45 minutes. Add the parsley, cook for 2 minutes and serve hot.

*Serving suggestions:* Serve with *Rice croquettes* (see page 56), *Arame, onions and dried daikon* (see page 124) and a boiled salad of white cabbage and sauerkraut (see page 115 on how to prepare boiled salads).

## Split Pea Pâté

Serves 6.

*450 g/1 lb green split peas, 15 cm/6 inch strip of kombu, 2 litres/$3\frac{1}{2}$ pt water, 6 medium carrots, 4 medium onions, 2 tablespoons barley miso or white miso, 3 teaspoons ginger juice (squeezed from freshly grated ginger)*

Wash the split peas and soak overnight in 1 litre/2 pt water. Soak the kombu for 1 hour in 290 ml/$\frac{1}{2}$ pt water. Cut the kombu into very fine strips and then dice these. Put the kombu and kombu soaking water into a heavy-bottomed saucepan. Add the split peas and soaking water, add 860 ml/$1\frac{1}{2}$ pt more water and simmer gently for $1\frac{1}{4}$ hours. Blend the miso in a little water and add to the peas with a little more water if necessary.

Dice the onions finely and grate the carrots. Add water to a frying pan to a depth of $\frac{1}{2}$ cm/$\frac{1}{4}$ inch, bring to a boil and add the diced onion. Turn to a medium heat and simmer for 5 minutes. Cooking onions on their own takes some of the acidic element out of them and makes them more digestible.

Add the grated carrot and a little water if necessary. Water sauté the carrot and onion for 15 minutes until they are sweet and dry. Add the vegetables to the split peas, then cook on a gentle heat for 15 minutes more. Stir in the ginger juice.

Blend the split peas to a smooth creamy texture in a blender or suribachi. Press firmly into a suitably sized pyrex loaf dish or other square mould and allow at least 2 hours for the pâté to cool and set before serving.

*Serving suggestions:* Serve in pitta bread with sauerkraut or on rice or wheat crackers with a *Red radish and cucumber pressed salad* (see page 120).

### TOFU

Tofu is a soya bean product, high in protein and free from animal fat. It can be a good replacement for a light cream cheese if it is prepared with miso.

## Tofu Cheese

Serves 4.

*450 g/1 lb firm tofu, 2 tablespoons barley or rice miso, 2 tablespoons finely diced onion, ½ bunch chives or 3 to 4 spring onions, chopped*

Steam the tofu with a pinch of salt for 15 minutes. Remove the tofu and let it drain on some cheesecloth or kitchen towel. Blend the miso with 150 ml/¼ pt water and spread this miso paste on top of the tofu. Place in a refrigerator for 1 to 3 days.

Blend the miso and tofu to a firm creamy texture in a suribachi or blender. Add the onion or chives and let the cheese sit for at least 1 hour before serving. Whirl the tofu cheese into a round and serve with a garnish of finely chopped chives.

*Serving suggestions:* Serve as a dip for bread and crackers, as a salad dressing or as the filling for some pastry cups which have been baked blind.

## Tofu Age

Serves 6.

*340 g/12 oz firm tofu, 3 × 15 cm/6 inch strips of kombu, 3 small onions, 2 tablespoons umeboshi paste (or 3 umeboshi plums), 1 to 2 tablespoons wholewheat flour, to bind if necessary, sesame or sunflower oil for deep-frying*

Wipe the excess salt from the kombu strips with a clean damp cloth and soak for 1 hour in water to cover. Remove the kombu onto kitchen towel and allow it to drain thoroughly. Mash the tofu and mix with the umeboshi paste. If necessary add some of the flour to make the tofu firm enough to make small balls in your hands.

Cut the kombu into very fine strips and mix with the tofu. Dice the onions finely and add to the tofu just before frying. Press the tofu mixture into small balls with your hands.

Add oil to a depth of about 5 cm/2 inches in a saucepan and heat. When the oil is hot enough, a small piece of vegetable dropped into it will immediately rise sizzling to the surface. The correct temperature is very important in successful deep-frying. Drop the balls into the oil 2 or 3 at a time and deep-fry until golden. Remove onto kitchen towel to drain, then arrange in an attractive serving dish.

*Serving suggestions:* Tofu age makes a decorative party food that can be arranged attractively on a tray and eaten with the fingers. Something sour tasting like pickles or sauerkraut will aid in the digestion of the oil.

## Tofu Spread

Serves 4.

*450 g/1 lb firm tofu, 15 cm/6 inch strip of kombu, 170 g/6 oz pumpkin seeds, 3 tablespoons white miso, 1 tablespoon rice vinegar, ¼ cucumber*

Steam the tofu for 10 minutes on a high heat with the kombu underneath. Kombu adds minerals and flavour to the tofu.

Wash the pumpkin seeds in a sieve and dry roast them on a medium heat until they pop and turn golden. Blend the seeds in a coffee grinder or suribachi and set them aside for use later.

Wash the cucumber and dice into very small cubes. Blend the tofu in a suribachi or blender with the white miso and rice vinegar. Blend in the pumpkin seeds and the cucumber, keeping some aside for a garnish.

*Serving suggestions:* Serve as a dip for crackers or place a dollop inside a lettuce leaf and garnish with chives or a sprinkling of finely chopped oregano.

## Scrambled Tofu

Serves 2.

*450 g/1 lb firm tofu, 4 tablespoons sesame oil, 7 medium sized onions, 2 tablespoons barley miso, 570 ml/1 pt water, 2 teaspoons ginger juice (squeezed from freshly grated ginger root), 4 spring onions*

Cut the onions into thin half-moons (see page 42). Heat the oil in a skillet and add the onion. Sauté for 5 to 10 minutes on a low heat, adding a little water if necessary to prevent burning. Crumble the tofu between your fingers into a bowl and layer it on top of the onions. Cook for 5 minutes.

Blend the miso with a little water and mix with the tofu and onion. Turn the heat very low and cook for 3 minutes. Then add the ginger juice. Cut the spring onions finely on the diagonal, add to the tofu and cook for 1 minute before serving. Garnish with a sprig of parsley.

*Serving suggestions:* For a light meal scrambled tofu is delicious served over a bowl or plate of noodles. Add a little umeboshi paste mixed with rice vinegar as a dressing for extra zest or a little finely chopped cucumber.

## FISH

Fish is a very good source of protein. Generally white fleshed fish is a better source of protein than red meat fish because it is less oily and more digestible.

### Deep-fried Cod with Green Pepper Dressing

Serves 6.

*6 × 170 g/6 oz cod steaks, 60 g/2 oz arrowroot powder, 8 tablespoons shoyu, sesame or sunflower oil for deep frying, 2 small green peppers, 3 tablespoons sesame oil, 2½ tablespoons white miso, 290 ml/½ pt water, 1 teaspoon arrowroot powder, 1 teaspoon kuzu powder*

Baste the cod steaks with the shoyu and allow them to sit for half an hour.

Add the oil to a saucepan to a depth of 7.5 cm/3 inches or 10 cm/4 inches and heat. When the oil is hot enough, a small piece of vegetable dropped into it will quickly come sizzling to the surface. Roll the cod steaks in the arrowroot powder and deep-fry 1 or 2 at a time until they are crisp and golden. After frying place them on kitchen towel to absorb excess oil. Place on individual plates or on a large serving dish and keep warm.

To make the dressing, cut the seeds out of the peppers and slice them thinly from end to end into fine matchsticks. Heat the oil in a frying pan or skillet and sauté the pepper on a medium heat for 5 or 6 minutes. Blend the white miso in 150 ml/¼ pt of the water and add to the pepper. Blend the arrowroot in 75 ml/⅛ pt of water, add to the pan and cook for 1 minute. Blend the kuzu in the remaining water and add this to the pan. After cooking for 1 or 2 minutes more pour the sauce over the fish. Add a garnish of mustard cress and a slice of lemon if desired.

*Variations:* When making the dressing, sauté diced onions for 5 minutes before adding the green pepper. This will give the dish a sweeter flavour.

*Serving suggestions:* Serve with a *Leek and umeboshi noodle salad* (see page 71) and cauliflower *Brine pickles* (see page 132).

## Whiting with Tofu and Onion Sauce

Serves 6.

*6 × 170 g/6 oz pieces of whiting fillet (ling steak or fillet can also be used), 8 tablespoons shoyu, 6 onions, 450 g/1 lb firm tofu, 2-3 drops shoyu, 15 cm/6 inch strip of kombu, 3 tablespoons white miso, 3 teaspoons ginger juice (squeezed from freshly grated ginger), 110 g/4 oz chopped parsley, 60 g/2 oz flaked almonds to garnish*

Marinate the whiting fillets in the shoyu for at least half an hour (preferably an hour).

Begin making the sauce by peeling the onions and cutting into fine half moons (see page 42). Place the kombu on the bottom of a frying pan, add the onions and a 1 cm/½ inch of water. Cover and steam the onions for 20 to 30 minutes, adding a little more water if necessary. Add 85 g/3 oz chopped parsley and cook a further 5 minutes. Blend the white miso in a little water, add to the onions and cook for 1 to 2 minutes. Add the ginger juice, take the pan off the heat and set aside.

Steam the tofu blocks in a steaming basket or with a ½ cm/¼ inch of water in a saucepan, with a few drops of shoyu for 10 to 15 minutes. Remove the blocks and blend in a blender with the onion and parsley.

Grill the fish gently for about 4 minutes on either side. Serve the fish with the tofu and onion sauce poured over and garnish with the remaining chopped parsley and the flaked almonds lightly roasted.

*Serving suggestions:* Serve with slices of *Millet loaf* (see page 59), a *Spring greens and sunflower seed salad* (see page 116) and whole steamed onions.

### Ling with Almond and Ginger Sauce

Serves 6.

*6 × 170 g/6 oz fillets of ling, 3 tablespoons shoyu, 170 g/6 oz whole almonds, 60 g/2 oz flaked almonds, lightly roasted, 4 spring onions, finely chopped, 4 teaspoons ginger juice (squeezed from freshly grated ginger root), 1 litre/2 pt water or vegetable stock, 1 pinch of sea salt, 2 tablespoon arrowroot powder*

Wash the ling fillets and cut them into 2.5 cm/1 inch cubes. Sprinkle with the shoyu and allow to sit for at least half an hour.

Wash the whole almonds and dry roast under a grill or in an oven. Grind them to a powder in a coffee grinder. The flavour of freshly ground almonds is much richer than that of bought ground almonds. Heat the water or vegetable stock in a pan. Add the salt, ginger juice and ground almonds to the water. Blend the arrowroot to a thin paste in a little cold water, take the almond sauce off the heat and stir in the arrowroot. Replace the sauce on the heat and simmer gently for 10 minutes, stirring constantly until the sauce has thickened. Use a flame tamer if necessary to prevent the sauce catching at the bottom.

Heat a frying pan or skillet with a ½cm/¼ inch water and add the ling. Cook on a gentle heat for about 5 minutes, until the ling is tender. Add the shoyu marinade and cook for another minute. Place the ling on individual plates and pour the sauce decoratively over. Garnish with the flaked almonds and spring onions.

*Serving suggestions:* For a simple meal serve with a *Noodle, carrot flower and broccoli floret salad* (see page 70).

### Fried Cod with Shitake Mushroom Sauce

Serves 6.

*6 × 170 g/6 oz servings of cod fillet or steak, 8 tablespoons shoyu, 6 to 8 tablespoons sesame oil, 6 shitake (dried mushrooms), 1 litre/2 pt water, 2 tablespoons kuzu, 4 tablespoons shoyu, 6 gherkins or 60 g/2 oz chopped parsley for garnish*

Wash the cod fillets or steaks and drain well. Sprinkle with the shoyu and allow them to marinate for at least half an hour before cooking. If possible marinate for several hours, particularly with steaks.

Soak the shitake mushrooms in 290 ml/½ pt water for 20 minutes. Heat the 1 litre/2 pt water and the shitake soaking water. Cut off the stalks of the mushrooms, which are too tough to eat but which can be saved for making soup stock. Cut the mushroom heads into very fine strips. Simmer these in the water for 8 minutes, then add the shoyu and cook for 2 more minutes. Blend the kuzu in 3 to 4 tablespoons of cold water, remove the pan from the heat, and stir in the kuzu. Return the pan to the heat and stir for several minutes until the sauce has thickened.

Heat a frying pan, add the sesame oil, and fry the drained cod pieces gently for about 4 minutes on either side. Add a little of the shoyu marinade a couple of minutes before the end of cooking. Serve the cod with the sauce poured over, garnished with the gherkins cut into *Gherkin fans* (see page 135) or with the parsley.

*Serving suggestions:* Serve with *Millet and almond pasta rolls* (see page 63) and steamed kale. A raw *Carrot and cucumber salad* (see page 120) would balance the meal well.

### Hake with Thyme Sauce

Serves 6.

*6 × 170 g/6 oz servings hake (or cod fillet or steak), 12 tablespoons shoyu, 720 ml/1¼ pt water, 6 teaspoons dried thyme, ½ cucumber, cut into fine slices, juice of ½ lemon, 2 tablespoons kuzu*

Wash the hake and skin it if necessary. Sprinkle shoyu over the fish and allow the fish to marinate in the shoyu for at least half an hour before cooking.

When the fish has marinated, pour off the shoyu and fish oils into a heavy-bottomed frying pan. Add the thyme, lemon juice and water and allow the mixture to sit for 20 minutes before cooking the fish. Then heat the liquid and poach the hake for 4 to 5 minutes on a low heat with a lid. After about 5 minutes the fish flesh should be white but not crumbly. Take out the fish with a fish slice and place on a serving plate over a bed of delicately arranged cucumber slices. Keep warm. Save 3 or 4 slices of cucumber to garnish each fillet or steak.

Blend the kuzu in a little cold water and take the fish cooking juice off the heat. Add the kuzu, replace on a low heat and stir constantly until the sauce has thickened. Pour a little of the sauce over each individual serving of fish. Garnish with the remaining cucumber slices and serve.

*Serving suggestion:* Serve with a *Red radish and cucumber pressed salad* (see page 120) and shell noodles.

## Cod Brightling

Serves 6.

*6 × 170 g/6 oz servings of cod fillet (ling or hake will substitute nicely), 8 tablespoons sake or mirin, 14 tablespoons shoyu, 1 lemon, ½ cup roasted sunflower seeds or pinenuts to garnish, 1 tablespoon kuzu*

Wash the cod and remove the skin. Mix the mirin and shoyu together, pour over the fish and marinate for 1 to 2 hours. Then drain the fish, reserving the marinade.

Put 1 cm/½ inch of water in a large saucepan and insert a steaming basket or metal collander. Place a piece of muslin across the inside of the basket (this is not absolutely necessary if you have not got any). Put the fish in the basket, cover with a well-fitting lid and steam for 5 minutes. Put the fish on serving plates and keep warm.

Pour the shoyu and mirin marinade into a pan, add a couple of drops of lemon juice and heat. Blend the kuzu in 1 to 2 tablespoons of cold water, take the marinade off the heat and stir in the kuzu. Replace on the heat and cook until the sauce thickens, stirring gently all the time. Pour the sauce over the cod and garnish liberally with the roasted pine nuts or sunflower seeds. Place a thin slice of lemon decoratively beside the fish.

*Serving suggestions:* Serve with *Deep fried millet balls* (see page 62) — 2 or 3 per person and boiled brussels sprouts with a grated carrot and onion salad with *Mustard miso dressing* (see page 131).

## Turbot Pâté

Serves 6.

*6 × 170 g/6 oz portions of turbot (halibut or hake can also be used), 2 cloves of garlic, 8 tablespoons shoyu, 1 tablespoon spring onions, finely cut on the diagonal, 6 medium onions, 3 medium carrots, 450 g/1 lb firm tofu, 1 tablespoon agar agar flakes, 3 teaspoons dried sage, 1 tablespoon umeboshi paste (optional), 2 tablespoons kuzu powder, 1 bunch parsley heads, 60 g/20 oz roasted sesame seeds, 1 lemon*

Peel the garlic cloves and cut finely, then mix them with the shoyu. Skin the fish, pour the garlic and shoyu marinade over them and sprinkle the cut spring onions on top of the fish. Leave to marinate for just 30 minutes.

Place the fish with the marinade juice and 150 ml/¼ pt water in a large frying pan or skillet. Simmer gently for 5 to 10 minutes, depending on the thickness of the fish. When the fish is cooked, mash it gently with a fork and put it in a bowl and set aside for later.

Bring 1 litre/2 pints water to a boil. Dice the onions and boil for 5 minutes. Grate the carrots, add to the onion, and simmer gently for a further minute. Crumble the tofu into small pieces between your fingers into the pan. Allow to simmer for 5 minutes then add the agar agar flakes, sage and umeboshi paste if desired. Simmer for 10 minutes on a very low heat, preferably using a flame tamer. Blend the kuzu in 3 to 4 tablespoons of cold water, remove the tofu mixture from the heat, stir in the kuzu and cook again until it thickens.

Layer the parsley heads (saving a few for garnish) in a bed at the bottom of a glass dish and pour the tofu mixture over the parsley. When this mixture is half set, put it into a blender together with the turbot and blend to a creamy consistency. Put in a simple glass serving dish or individual ramekins and garnish with parsley, roasted sesame seeds and a slim wedge of lemon.

*Variations:* This fish dish works well served as a flan on a bed of couscous. For extra flavour and for visual appeal, place a ring of fresh peeled prawns around the outside of the flan.

## Sole Marinade

Serves 4.

*4 medium fillets lemon sole, 4 tablespoons mirin or cider vinegar, 4 tablespoons shoyu, 2 to 4 tablespoons water, 110 g/4 oz mushrooms, sliced, 4 spring onions, finely chopped, 60 g/2 oz parsley, finely chopped*

Place the sole fillets in a bowl. Mix the mirin or cider vinegar, shoyu and water together to form a marinade. Pour this over the fish and marinate for 2 to 4 hours. Use enough water in the marinade, so that it completely covers the fish.

Heat a frying pan and add the sliced mushrooms. Dry roast on a medium heat for 2 to 3 minutes. Cut the sole fillets in 2.5 cm/1 inch strips and add with the marinade to the mushrooms. Simmer for 2 to 3 minutes. Add the spring onions and simmer for 1 to 2 minutes more. Garnish with the parsley and serve.

# 10. VEGETABLE DISHES

### Carrot Chunks in Miso and Ginger

Serves 4.

*4 to 6 large carrots (or 2 to 3 burdock roots), 3 tablespoons sesame oil, 3 tablespoons barley miso, 190 ml/⅓ pt water, 2 tablespoons ginger juice (squeezed from freshly grated ginger)*

Wash the carrots and cut into 1 cm/½ inch thick rounds. If burdock is available, use it instead. Heat the oil in a heavy-bottomed frying pan. Add the carrots and fry for 10 minutes on either side, keep the heat low, otherwise the carrots will burn. The longer you cook the carrots, the richer and more warming and strengthening the dish.

Blend the miso in the water to a smooth consistency in a suribachi or cup and add to the carrots. Cook for about 6 minutes until the miso sauce has nearly dried out. Add the ginger juice and cook a minute longer before serving hot.

*Variations:* 2 tablespoons of mirin or sake can be used instead of or as well as the ginger. A few finely chopped spring onions can be added as garnish.

*Serving suggestions:* This dish is best served with whole grains, such as *Rice and sweet rice* (see page 55). It is nice served with steamed greens and cauliflower *Brine pickles* (see page 132). Alternatively serve it with *Deep fried tempeh fingers* (see page 80) and sauerkraut.

## Onion Butter

Serves 6.

*12 medium sized onions, 860 ml/1½ pt water, 3 tablespoons barley miso, 1 pinch of sea salt*

Place 290 ml/½ pt water in a heavy-bottomed saucepan, add the pinch of sea salt and bring to a boil. Cut the onions into half moons (see page 42) and add to the pan. Place a lid on the saucepan, turn the heat to medium for 5 minutes and then very low for 1 hour, adding a little more water as necessary to prevent burning.

After an hour, remove the lid and cook until no liquid remains. Put the onions in a suribachi and blend them to a creamy consistency. Add the miso and blend it in.

*Serving suggestions:* Serve onion butter hot as part of a main meal, or serve on crackers or rice cakes. Onion butter goes really well with *Millet loaf* (see page 59) and *Lentil pate* (see page 85) with a garnish of spring onions and a salad.

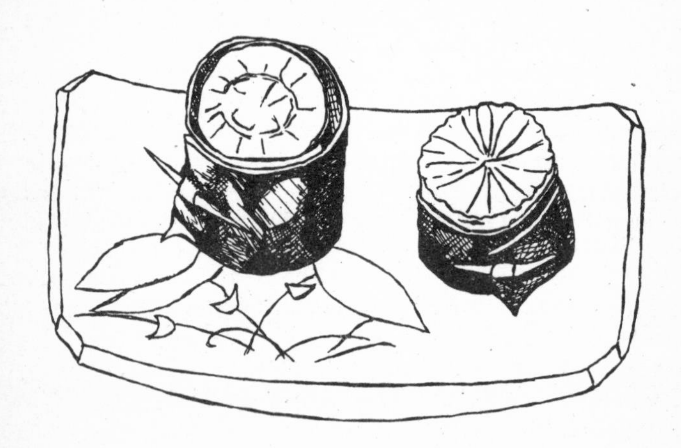

## Nishime Carrots and Yellow Turnips

Serves 6.

*8 large carrots, 3 turnips, 2 bunches fresh watercress, 2 × 15 cm/6 inch strips of kombu, 1 pinch of sea salt, 2 tablespoons shoyu*

Wash the vegetables and wipe the salt rime from the kombu with a damp cloth. Soak the kombu in water to cover for 1 hour.

After the kombu has soaked, cut it into 2.5 cm/1 inch squares and place it at the bottom of a heavy-based saucepan —

enamelled iron is very suitable cookware for this dish. Cut the turnips into thick half moons (see page 42) and place on top of the kombu. Cut the carrots into irregular chunks and spread on top. Add water to a third of the way up the vegetables and the pinch of sea salt.

Bring the vegetables to a boil on a high heat, turn to medium and simmer for 20 minutes. Add a little more water if necessary to prevent burning, but don't swamp the vegetables. Add the shoyu and simmer 5 minutes more. Cut the watercress into 1 cm/½ inch lengths and sprinkle over the top of the carrots. Replace the lid and cook for 1 minute. Serve this dish fresh and hot. If it is reheated it loses its zest and sparkle.

*Variations:* Try the recipe with other vegetables — carrot, swede and brussels sprouts; carrot, whole onions, seitan, and spring onion; carrot, parsnip and tofu; or carrot, onion and fu.

## Dried Daikon, Carrot and Kombu

Serves 6.

*2 × 15 cm/6 inch strips of kombu, 6 carrots, ¾ packet dried daikon, 2 tablespoons shoyu*

Wipe the salt rime from the kombu with a clean damp cloth and soak in water to cover for 1 hour. This makes the kombu softer and more edible. Briefly rinse the dried daikon and soak for 5 minutes in water to cover. Remove the kombu from the soaking water and cut it into thin 2.5 cm/1 inch strips. Place the kombu on the bottom of a heavy-based saucepan and add the dried daikon and the soaking water from both the kombu and the daikon (unless the daikon soaking water is very dark brown in which case it should be discarded). Cut the carrot into fine matchsticks and spread it on top of the daikon.

Simmer the carrot and daikon and kombu on a medium heat for 10 minutes, then turn the heat low and simmer for a further 25 minutes. If necessary add a little water to prevent burning. Add the shoyu and cook 5 minutes longer. Remove the lid and allow any liquid left in the pan to cook away, then serve.

*Variations:* Dried daikon and kombu can be cooked together without the carrot. Aother delicious dish is 50 per cent onions and 50 per cent dried daikon cooked together with kombu. All these are very warming and hearty dishes.

*Serving suggestions:* Serve for an evening meal together with whole grains and steamed brussels sprouts or kale.

## Marinated Onions and Brussels Sprouts

Serves 6.

*18 pickling onions, 24 small brussels sprouts, 290 ml/½ pt umeboshi vinegar, 290 ml/½ pt water*

Wash and peel the onions and brussels sprouts. Cut a cross through the stem of the brussels sprouts to a depth of ½ cm/¼ inch. Bring about 860 ml/1½ pt water to a rolling boil. Add the onions and boil them for 5 minutes, then remove with a slotted spoon. Repeat with the brussels sprouts and place both together in a glass or ceramic serving dish. Mix the water and umeboshi vinegar together and marinate the onions and brussels sprouts in it for at least 2 hours. Before serving, pour off the marinade and keep for use in a dressing or other dish. This is a good dish to prepare in the morning and to leave to marinate until the evening.

*Serving suggestions:* This is a good dish to serve with an otherwise long-cooked or baked meal, such as with *Tofu lasagne* (see page 73), pressure cooked *Rice and sweet rice* (see page 55), or with fish or a pie. This dish would also be lovely blended and served with a garnish of carrot flowers inside a rolled up *Sourdough Pancake* (see page 74).

## Water Sauté Onions

Serves 6.

*8 medium onions, 1 tablespoon rice syrup, 1 tablespoon shoyu*

Cut the onions into fine half moons (see page 42). Heat 290 ml/½ pt water to boiling in a heavy-bottomed frying pan or skillet, add the onion and turn the heat to medium low. Simmer the onions for 25 minutes, stirring occasionally. Add a little more water to just keep the bottom of the pan covered, but don't add too much as this destroys the delicate sweet flavour of the onions.

After 25 minutes add the shoyu and cover the pan. Do not add any more liquid after this stage of preparation. After 3 minutes add the rice syrup and mix among the onions, then turn off the heat. Allow the onions to sit with the rice syrup with the lid off the frying pan for a few minutes — this makes the flavour sweeter and more delicious. This dish is deliciously sweet and relaxing.

*Variations:* Carrots can be cooked 50:50 with the onions for variety, or pumpkin can be cooked with carrot in the same way. Children love these sweet-tasting vegetable dishes.

*Serving suggestions:* Good as a lunchtime or evening vegetable accompaniment to *Couscous loaf* (see page 65). It can also be puréed with some cucumber or mustard cress to make a vegetable spread for rice cakes or crackers.

## Swede and Carrot Sticks

Serves 6.

*1 swede, 6 large carrots, 1 pinch of sea salt, 110 g/4 oz rice flakes, 450 g/1 lb pumpkin or squash (a sweeter variety such as hokkaido, buttercup or acorn) or carrots or onions, 150 ml/¼ pt umeboshi vinegar, 860 ml/1½ pt water, spring onions to garnish*

Heat 570 ml/1 pt water and add a pinch of sea salt. Cut the carrots and swede into large matchsticks 5 to 7.5 cm/2 to 3 inches long and ½ cm/¼ inch thick. The sticks must be thick enough so that they can be used to scoop up the dip sauce. Blanch the carrot and swede for 1 minute in the water. Remove and cool in a sieve or collander under cold, running water. Arrange attractively in a glass or on a tray and serve with the dip sauce below.

For the dip sauce, bring 570 ml/1 pt water to a boil in a heavy-bottomed frying pan. Dice the pumpkin into small cubes and simmer for 10 minutes. Add the rice flakes and the remaining water and simmer for a further 10 minutes on a low heat, preferably with a flame tamer. Cover the frying pan with a lid to prevent too much evaporation of the cooking liquid. Add the umeboshi vinegar, replace the lid and cook for 10 minutes more. To obtain a creamy consistency, blend the pumpkin and rice flakes with a blender or suribachi. Serve in an attractive dish and add a few spring onions for garnish.

*Variations:* This dish is a colourful party favourite. Other shapes can be used — swede triangles or oblongs and carrot fans or flowers. Sticks are quick and simple to make for a family evening meal. You can also use other dip sauces, such as *Sunset dip* (see page 141) or *Tofu spread* (see page 142).

*Serving suggestions:* Serve at parties, as an hors d'oeuvre for a dinner party, as a snack for children and adults or as part of a picnic lunch in the garden. The vegetables and dip sauce would compliment something more substantial like grain burgers e.g. *Rice croquettes* (see page 56) or *Millet and lentil burgers* (see page 60).

## Grated Carrot and Parsley Sauté

Serves 6.

*6 to 8 medium carrots, 110 g/4 oz parsley, 150 ml/¼ pt water, 3 tablespoons sesame oil, 225 g/8 oz pumpkin seeds, 1 tablespoon umeboshi vinegar (or ½ tablespoon shoyu and ½ tablespoon rice vinegar), 1 tablespoon shoyu*

Wash and finely grate the carrots and chop the parsley finely. Heat a frying pan and add the sesame oil. When the oil is hot add the grated carrot and turn the heat medium low. Sauté the carrots for 10 minutes, then add 150 ml/¼ pt water to prevent sticking. Bring the water to a simmer, add the shoyu and sauté the carrot for 2 minutes more. Add the parsley and sauté for 2 minutes before placing in a serving dish.

Meanwhile dry roast the pumpkin seeds until they pop and turn golden. At the end of cooking sprinkle with the umeboshi vinegar. Return the seeds to the heat for 1 minute so that they become crisp and dry again. Sprinkle over the carrot and parsley sauté.

*Variations:* There are endless variations on this theme. Precooked seitan or tempeh can be added to the carrots. Precooked noodles can be mixed in at the end to make a more complete meal — if they are wheels, shells or whirls, they really enhance the decorative appeal of the dish.

*Serving suggestions:* For a light lunch, serve on a bed of wholewheat spaghetti or udon noodles with a side salad of blanched broccoli with *Tahini shoyu sauce* (see page 130).

## Carrots and Chestnuts with Miso Sauce

Serves 6.

*6 to 8 carrots, 1 pinch of sea salt, 225 g/8 oz dried chestnuts, 15 cm/6 inch strip of kombu, 1 tablespoon shoyu, 2 tablespoons white miso, 60 g/2 oz kuzu, 1 tablespoon ginger juice (squeezed from fresh grated ginger), fine slithers of spring onion or finely chopped parsley to garnish*

Rinse and soak the dried chestnuts overnight in enough water to cover.

Wipe the salt rime from the kombu with a clean damp cloth and place in the bottom of a pressure cooker. Add the chestnuts, chestnut soaking water, and another 1 litre/2 pt water. Add the shoyu and pressure cook for 20 minutes. If you do not have a pressure cooker boil the chestnuts for 1 hour, adding shoyu after 30 minutes. Pressure cooking makes the chestnuts more flavourful and more digestible. Place the chestnuts in the centre of a large serving dish and keep the chestnut cooking water for making the sauce.

Bring 570 ml/1 pt water to a boil in a heavy-bottomed frying pan or saucepan and add the pinch of sea salt. Cut the carrots into fine matchsticks and simmer on a low heat for 10 minutes or until all the water has gone. Place the carrot matchsticks decoratively around the outside of the chestnuts on the serving dish. Keep the chestnuts and carrots warm while making the sauce.

Place the chestnut cooking water in a saucepan and bring to a simmer. Blend the kuzu with the minimum of cold water to make a paste. Take the chestnut water from the heat and stir in the kuzu. Return the pan to the heat and stir gently until the kuzu thickens. If it becomes too thick, add a little water to get it to a sauce consistency. Take a little of the sauce out of the pan, blend the white miso in it, and stir this into the chestnut sauce. Add the ginger juice and pour the sauce over the chestnuts and a little over the carrots as a glaze. Sprinkle with spring onions to garnish.

*Serving suggestions:* This dish makes a lovely autumn and winter dish. It also makes a decorative Christmas dish. It could be served with *Millet Loaf* (see page 59), steamed chinese cabbage and baked parsnips.

### Baked Onions Stuffed with Green Pepper and Miso

Serves 6.

*5 to 7 large onions, 2 green peppers, 2 tablespoons sesame oil, 3 tablespoons barley miso, 15 cm/6 inch strip of kombu, ½ packet of dried mochi, 1 tablespoon freshly grated ginger juice, spring onions or parsley to garnish*

Cut the top and bottom off the onions and peel them but leave whole. Wipe the salt rime from the kombu with a clean, damp cloth and place the kombu at the bottom of a cooking pot. Put the onions on top. The kombu sea vegetable greatly enhances the flavour of the onions because of its high mineral content. Add enough water to cover the onions and bring to a boil. Turn the heat to medium low and simmer for 50 minutes.

Remove the onions onto a plate and allow them to cool. It is always advisable to do at least one extra onion, as one often breaks when they are being stuffed. Remove the centre of the onions by first pressing with a chopstick and then with the end of a large, wooden cooking spoon. The centre of the onion should come away quite easily leaving the onion free for stuffing.

Heat a heavy-bottomed frying pan and add the sesame oil. Cut the green peppers into fine matchsticks and sauté them for 5 minutes. Blend 2 tablespoons of the miso with 2 tablespoons of water, add to the green pepper, and sauté on a very low heat for 1 minute. Stuff the green pepper condiment into the centre of each onion with a little sticking out, and place the onions on a baking tray.

Grate or chop the dried mochi into very thin slithers. Bring 570 ml/1 pt water to a boil in a pan and add the mochi. Simmer on a low heat for 10 to 15 minutes until the mochi has dissolved into a thick sauce. Add more water if necessary. Blend the remaining 1 tablespoon of miso in 1 or 2 tablespoons of water and add to the mochi. Add the ginger juice and cook for a minute.

Pour this sauce over the onions to make a thick glaze and put them in a pre-heated oven at 190°C/375°F/Gas Mark 5. Cook for at least 25 minutes until the mochi turns crisp and golden. Serve piping hot.

## Baked Onions with Sesame Couscous

Serves 6.

*5 to 7 large onions, 2 tablespoons sesame oil, 3 tablespoons barley miso, 15 cm/6 inch strip of kombu, 170 g/6 oz couscous, 170 g/6 oz grated carrot, 570 ml/1 pt water, 110 g/4 oz sesame seeds, 2 tablespoons finely chopped parsley*

Peel and cook the onions as in the previous recipe, then remove their centres.

Wash the couscous in a sieve under a tap and drain. Heat a heavy-bottomed frying pan and add the oil. When the oil is hot add the couscous and sauté it on a medium heat until it is golden. Grate the carrot, add it to the couscous and sauté for 3 to 4 minutes until the carrots are soft and sweet.

Blend 2 tablespoons of the miso with 150 ml/¼ pt water and add to the couscous with the remaining water. Cover the couscous with a well-fitting lid and steam for 3 minutes. Remove the pan from the heat and leaving the lid on, allow the couscous to continue cooking for a further 10 minutes in its own heat. Then add the chopped parsley.

Wash and drain the sesame seeds then dry roast in a frying pan. When they crush easily when rubbed between the thumb and third finger they are done. Remove the seeds and blend to a powder in a coffee grinder or suribachi. Mix the sesame seeds with the couscous then stuff the mixture into the onions.

Grill for about 10 minutes on a medium setting or bake for about 25 minutes in the middle of the oven at 190°C/375°F/Gas Mark 5, until crisp on the outside.

*Variations:* The onions can also be stuffed with rice flakes, bulghur or millet instead of couscous, but these grains need a longer cooking time. If the bulghur is pre-soaked each of these grains can cook in 35 minutes. Arame sea vegetable, diced onion, mustard and ginger can be added to the basic recipe. For a more crunchy texture add whole or chopped sunflower seeds or pumpkin seeds and a garnish of flaked almonds. Dry roast the seeds or almonds first.

### Swede Cups

Serves 6.

*4 to 6 small swedes, 15 cm/6 inch strip of kombu, 170 g/6 oz rice flakes, 1 litre/2 pt water, 60 g/2 oz dulse flakes or finely chopped dulse, 3 to 4 onions, 1 tablespoon sesame oil, 60 g/2 oz finely chopped parsley, 1 tablespoon barley miso, 1 teaspoon ginger juice (squeezed from freshly grated ginger)*

Wipe the kombu with a damp cloth to remove excess salt and place in the bottom of a large heavy-based saucepan. Wash, top and tail the swedes until they are a pleasant round shape and sit easily without rolling over. Place the swedes in the pan and add water to a third of their height. Steam the swedes for 50 minutes to 1 hour.

Bring 1 litre/2 pt water to a boil and add the rice flakes and dulse flakes. Turn the heat very low and cook gently for 30 minutes. Heat the oil in a heavy-bottomed frying pan. Dice the onions and sauté for 5 minutes until they are golden. Blend the miso with a few tablespoons of water and add to the onions. Turn the heat very low, simmer the onion and miso for 2 minutes, then add the ginger juice and the parsley. Mix the rice flakes and dulse with the onion sauté.

Take the swedes off the heat and allow them to cool sufficiently to be handled. Use a round soup spoon to scoop out the top half of each swede to form a cup. Stuff the cup with the rice flake and onion mixture.

*Serving suggestions:* Serve the swede cups with *Peanut sauce* (see page 129) or topped with mochi as in the recipe for *Baked onions stuffed with green pepper and miso* (see page 103).

## Kinpira Carrots

Serves 6.

*10 medium carrots, 4 tablespoons sesame oil, 2 tablespoons shoyu, 60 g/2 oz sesame seeds*

Wash and cut the carrots into medium sized matchsticks. Heat a large, heavy-bottomed frying pan, preferably cast iron which transfers heat well and doesn't burn the food easily. Heat the oil in the pan, add the carrot matchsticks and sauté on a high heat for 5 to 10 minutes. Add the shoyu and sauté for a further 2 to 3 minutes on a medium heat. The carrots should be cooked until they are sweet tasting but still crunchy. Take the carrots out of the pan and arrange them attractively on a glass, ceramic or wooden platter.

Roast the sesame seeds in a frying pan until golden and sprinkle over the carrots.

*Variations:* Carrot and burdock can be cooked together, using 2 times the quantity of carrots to burdock because burdock has a stronger flavour and masks the flavour of the carrot. Fry the burdock for 2 to 3 minutes before adding the carrot.

*Serving suggestions:* Serve with *Millet loaf* (see page 59) or *Rice and chestnuts* (see page 56) and a *Cabbage and watercress boiled salad* (see page 117).

## Baked Onions and Celery

Serves 6.

*6 carrots, 290 ml/½ pt umeboshi vinegar, 290 ml/½ pt water, 12 medium sized onions, 6 large stalks of celery, 3 tablespoons sesame oil, 1 tablespoon shoyu, 2 teaspoons ginger juice (squeezed from freshly grated ginger), ½ lemon*

Cut the carrots into matchsticks, blanch in boiling water for half a minute, then cool in a sieve under running water. Mix the umeboshi vinegar and water and marinate the carrot matchsticks in the marinade for at least 1 hour.

Peel the onions and place them whole on a baking tray. Cut each celery stick diagonally in half and place around the onions. Add a 1 cm/½ inch water to the tray and place in a preheated oven at 180°C/350°F/Gas Mark 4. Bake for 40 to 50 minutes, depending on the size of the onions. The onions should not be too soft or will break up when stuffed. After 20 minutes mix the shoyu, oil and ginger juice together and baste the onions and celery with it. Repeat the basting every 5 or 10 minutes until the onions are cooked.

Take the onions out of the oven and allow them to cool slightly. Remove the centres by pressing out with a chopstick or wooden spoon handle. Stuff the centres of the onion with a few marinated carrot matchsticks and serve the onions on a bed of marinated carrot matchsticks. Pour a little of the umeboshi vinegar marinade over each onion before serving. Serve the celery separately with a garnish of lemon juice.

*Serving suggestions:* Serve with whole grilled trout or *Sole marinade* (see page 96) and *Couscous loaf* (see page 65).

## Baked Cauliflower with Tofu Dressing

Serves 6.

*1 whole cauliflower, 225 g/8 oz firm tofu, 1 to 2 tablespoons miso, 60 g/2 oz sesame seeds, 1 tablespoon ready-made mustard*

Remove the leaves of the cauliflower, then place it in a large saucepan with a 1 cm/½ inch water. Cover and steam for 15 minutes. While the cauliflower is cooking, place the tofu in ½ cm/¼ inch water in a pan and steam for 10 minutes.

Wash the sesame seeds and roast in a frying pan on a medium heat, stirring frequently. When the seeds can be easily crushed between the thumb and third finger they are done. Grind the sesame seeds to a powder in a suribachi or coffee grinder. Mix the ground seeds and tofu together and blend to a cream in the suribachi or in a blender. Blend the miso in a little water and mix into the tofu and seeds. Then mix in the mustard.

Transfer the cauliflower onto a baking tray and spoon the tofu dressing over it. Bake in a preheated oven on a medium setting for 15 to 20 minutes, then serve.

*Variations:* Various dressings can be used over the cauliflower, including roasted and ground pumpkin seeds with ginger juice and shoyu; tahini, miso and lemon rind; or miso and rice vinegar.

### Baked Pumpkin, Swede, Parsnip or Carrot

Serves 6.

*1 medium sized sweet pumpkin such as hokkaido, buttercup or red kuri (or 675 g/1½ lb swede, parsnips or carrots), sesame oil to baste, 150 ml/¼ pt shoyu, 290 ml/½ pt water, 75 ml/⅛ pt ginger juice (squeezed from freshly grated ginger)*

Scrub the pumpkin and cut in half. Scoop out the seeds and set them aside (they are delicious fried with shoyu and rice vinegar). Cut the pumpkin end to end to make thick crescent-shaped pieces. Baste these with an oiled brush and place them on a large baking tray. Bake in a pre-heated oven at 200°C/400°F/Gas Mark 6 for about 40 minutes.

Mix the shoyu, water and ginger juice together to make a dip sauce for the pumpkin. Serve in 2 or 3 small bowls within everybody's reach.

If using swede, carrots and/or parsnips instead of pumpkin, cut the swede into quarters and the carrots and parsnips lengthways into quarters and boil for 5 to 10 minutes to make them more succulent. Then baste with the oil and bake for 30 to 40 minutes. Serve with the shoyu and ginger dip sauce.

### Tempura Vegetables

Serves 6.

*450 g/1 lb vegetables of 3 or 4 kinds, such as carrot, parsnip, cauliflower, broccoli, fresh mushrooms, onions, pumpkin and green pepper, sesame oil for deep frying, 225 g/8 oz 81 per cent wholewheat flour, 60 g/2 oz brown rice flour, 1 pinch of sea salt, 570 to 860 ml/1 to 1½ pt Perrier water, 4 tablespoons shoyu, 2 teaspoons ginger juice, 4 tablespoons water*

Make the batter by mixing the flours and salt together, then adding enough Perrier water to make a batter consistency. Let the batter sit for half an hour before using.

Cut the vegetables into thin slices or into florets. Heat the oil in a pan. When it is hot enough, a small piece of vegetable dropped into it will sink and then immediately rise sizzling to the surface. If the oil smokes, it is too hot. Dust the pieces of vegetable in a bowl of flour and then dip into the batter so that they become evenly coated.

Drop the vegetables into the oil 2 or 3 at a time. When they have become crisp and golden, spread them out on paper kitchen towel to absorb the excess oil. Repeat until all the vegetables are done. Make sure that the temperature of the oil doesn't drop, which will produce soggy tempura. You may need to allow the oil to heat up again between cooking each batch of vegetables.

Make a dip by mixing the shoyu, ginger juice and water together, and give each person a small bowl of it so that they can dip in their tempura as they eat it. Serve the tempura as quickly as possible, so that it doesn't loose its crispness.

### Pumpkin, Carrot and Leek Stew

Serves 6.

*8 large carrots, 450 g/1 lb orange pumpkin (for example hokkaido, red kuri, buttercup or acorn squash), 2 leeks, 15 cm/ 6 inch strip of kombu, 860 ml/1½ pt water, 1½ tablespoons kuzu, 2 tablespoons barley miso, 2 teaspoons ginger juice (squeezed from freshly grated ginger)*

Cut the carrots into half moons (see page 42) and the pumpkin into large cubes. Wipe the excess salt rime from the kombu with a damp cloth and place at the bottom of a heavy-based saucepan. Layer the carrots over the kombu and the pumpkin on top. Add 570 ml/1 pt water, cover and bring to a steam on a high heat, turn to medium and cook for 25 minutes. Add 190 ml/ ⅓ pt water and bring back to a simmer. Cut the leeks into thin diagonal slices, add to the stew and cook for 3 to 5 minutes.

Blend the miso in a little of the cooking juice, add to the stew and cook for 2 minutes. Dilute the kuzu in 75 ml/⅛ pt cold water, take the stew off the heat and gently stir in the kuzu. Return to the heat and stir until the liquid has thickened. Add the ginger juice and cook for 2 minutes and then serve.

*Serving suggestions:* Serve the stew hot with pitta bread and *Cabbage and watercress salad* (see page 117).

## Sweet 'n' Sour Carrots

Serves 6.

*8 carrots, cut into fine matchsticks, 4 onions, cut into fine half moons, 170 g/6 oz white cabbage diced, 8 spring onions, cut finely on the diagonal, 2 tablespoons shoyu, 5 tablespoons rice vinegar, 3 tablespoons rice syrup or mirin, 3 tablespoons sesame oil, 2 teaspoons kuzu, 150 ml/¼ pt water*

Wash and cut the vegetables. Heat a heavy-bottomed frying pan and add the oil. When the oil is hot add the onion and sauté until the onion is transparent. Add the carrot matchsticks and the diced white cabbage and sauté for 5 minutes. Add the shoyu and cook for 2 minutes. Blend the kuzu in the water, stir into the vegetables and cook for 2 minutes to glaze the vegetables. Then mix in the rice vinegar and rice syrup, cook 1 minute more and serve.

*Variations:* Carrots and onions are a good basis for this dish as they become very sweet. Instead of onions use swede, pumpkin or leek.

*Serving suggestions:* This makes a delicious filling for *Sourdough pancakes* (see page 74).

## Salsify and Carrot Sauté

Serves 4.

*1 large salsify root, cut in thin diagonal slices, 4 to 5 carrots, cut in thin matchsticks, 1 tablespoon sesame oil, 2 teaspoons shoyu*

Heat the oil in a frying pan on a medium heat. Sauté the salsify for 5 minutes. Add the carrots and cook for 3 minutes. Sprinkle the shoyu over the vegetables and cook 2 minutes longer. Serve immediately while the salsify and carrot are still crisp and hot.

## Carrot and Onion Purée

Serves 6.

*8 carrots, diced, 5 onions, diced, 570 ml/1 pt water, 2 bunches watercress, 225 g/8 oz sesame seeds, 1 teaspoon ginger juice (squeezed from freshly grated ginger), 1 tablespoon barley miso*

Bring 290 ml/½ pt water to a rolling boil in a heavy-bottomed frying pan, add the diced onions and stir-fry until they are transparent. Add the diced carrot, cover and simmer for 15 minutes. Add the remaining 290 ml/½ pt water as and when necessary.

Blend the miso with the minimum of water or vegetable stock to a runny paste and add this to the carrot and onion. Turn the heat very low and cook for 3 to 5 minutes — miso is best cooked very gently so that the living enzymes which help digestion are not killed by the heat. Wash and chop the watercress very finely, using the stems as well as the leaves. Spread the watercress on top of the carrot and onion, cover the pan and cook for 2 minutes. Then add the ginger juice, cook 1 minute more and turn off the heat.

Roast the sesame seeds in a frying pan until golden, then grind to a powder in a coffee mill. Blend the vegetables and powdered seeds in a blender or food mill. Place in a serving dish and add a sprig of watercress or a few unground sesame seeds for garnish.

## Cabbage d'Alsace

Serves 6.

*340 g/12 oz finely shredded white cabbage, 2 tablespoons sesame oil, 1 tablespoon shoyu, 2 tablespoons rice vinegar or cider vinegar, 110 g/4 oz sesame seeds*

Wash the sesame seeds in a sieve under a tap and drain. Heat a skillet or frying pan and dry roast the seeds on a medium heat for about 5 minutes, stirring continuously. When the sesame seeds are pale gold and crush easily when rubbed between the thumb and third finger they are ready. Take the seeds out of the pan and blend half in a coffee grinder. Mix the ground and unground seeds together.

Wash and cut the cabbage. Heat the oil in a large frying pan and sauté the cabbage for 6 to 7 minutes, stirring regularly with a wooden spoon. Add the shoyu, stir and cook for 2 minutes. Add the rice vinegar, sauté for 1 minute, then transfer to a serving dish and garnish with the roasted sesame seed mixture.

*Serving suggestions:* Serve with pressure cooked *Rice and aduki beans* (see page 55) and a grated carrot salad with *Mustard miso dressing* (see page 131).

## Dulse and Almond Medley

Serves 6.

*170 g/6 oz dulse, 6 carrots, cut into half moons (see page 00), 6 onions, diced, 110 g/4 oz whole almonds, 2 tablespoons shoyu, 425 ml/¾ pt water*

Wash the dulse in a sieve under running water, soak for 5 minutes in the water and then chop finely. Place the dulse at the bottom of a saucepan with the carrot half moons on top. Add the dulse soaking water and steam the carrot and dulse for 5 minutes. Spread the onions on top of the carrots and steam until all the water has been absorbed. Add the shoyu, turn the heat very low, and steam the dulse medley until all the water is gone. Take the medley out and arrange the vegetables decoratively on a serving dish.

Roast the almonds under the grill until golden but not dark brown. Cut each almond down its length into three or four slithers and mix the almonds with the dulse, onion and carrot. Serve hot or cold.

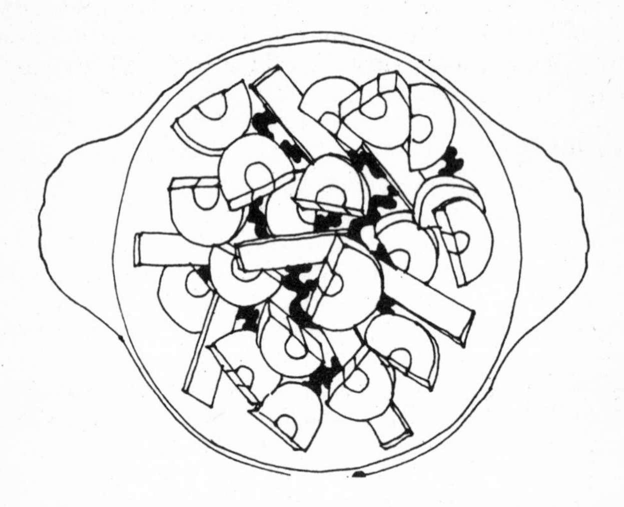

*Variations:* For a more economical and everyday dish serve the medley with dry roasted sesame, pumpkin or sunflower seeds. Filberts or hazelnuts will also work well for a richer taste. Ginger or a little lemon juice adds zest to this dish.

*Serving suggestions:* Serve with *Rice croquettes* (see page 56) and a *Spring greens and sunflower seed salad* (see page 116). This is an appetising and light lunch.

## Turnips with Ginger Sauce

Serves 6.

*6 medium sized turnips, 15 cm/6 inch strip of kombu cut into julienne strips, 2 tablespoons kuzu, 2 tablespoons barley miso, 1 tablespoon ginger juice (squeezed from freshly grated ginger)*

Choose the turnips with an aesthetically pleasing shape as they are going to be served whole. If people have a large appetite double the quantity of turnips, but one per person should be enough if there are several other dishes in the meal.

Soak the kombu in water to cover for 10 minutes, then cut it into very fine julienne strips and layer at the bottom of a heavy-based cooking pot. Place the whole turnips on top of the kombu, add the kombu soaking water plus 290 ml/½ pt water and steam the turnips for 15 to 20 minutes. Remove the turnips and place them decoratively on a serving dish.

Blend the kuzu in enough cold water to mix it to a paste. Take the turnip cooking water off the heat and stir in the kuzu. Replace this sauce on a low heat and stir until it thickens. Add a little more water if necessary. Add the ginger juice and simmer very gently for 1 minute, then pour the sauce over the turnips. Arrange the julienne strips of kombu attractively around the turnips.

## Miso Relish

Serves 6.

*2 carrots, cut in very fine matchsticks, 1 salsify or burdock root, cut in very fine matchsticks, 2 onions, cut in very fine half moons (see page 00), 1 tablespoon sesame oil, 1 tablespoon miso, 1 teaspoon ginger juice (squeezed from freshly grated ginger)*

Heat the oil in a frying pan on a medium heat and sauté the onion until it becomes transparent. Add the salsify or burdock matchsticks and sauté for 5 minutes. Add the carrots and sauté for 5 more minutes.

Blend the miso in a little water, add to the vegetables and cook for 5 minutes on a low heat. Add the ginger juice and continue to cook until the remaining liquid has cooked away.

This relish is quite strong, and so is used as a small side dish — about 2 tablespoons per person is plenty. It makes a lovely warming dish in the autumn and winter.

## Greens Rolls

Serves 6.

*18 large spring greens leaves, or soft cabbage leaves, 5 tablespoons tahini, 3 tablespoons umeboshi paste, 1 tablespoon lemon juice*

Wash the leaves and remove the hard central stalk by nicking out a V-shape from the base of the leaf. Mix the tahini, umeboshi paste and lemon juice together in a suribachi or blender to a smooth cream. Allow this dressing to sit while you prepare the leaves.

Bring 150 ml/¼ pt water to a boil, add the leaves, squashing them down if necessary. Cover the pot with a good fitting lid and steam for 4 to 5 minutes. Take the leaves out and spread them out on a plate to cool.

Take a sushi mat or similar undyed bamboo mat and cover with about 6 leaves so that they are at least two leaves thick all over. Spread a third of the tahini cream over the greens. Roll the greens leaves up in the sushi mat, pulling the edge of the mat back so that it doesn't get rolled up with the greens. Roll the greens as tightly as possible or the rolls will not stick together. When you have completely rolled the leaves up, wrap the suchi mat around them and squeeze the roll over the sink to get rid of excess water. Unroll the mat, making sure the greens stay tightly rolled, and cut into about 6 equal sections.

*Variations:* Fill the rolls with grated carrot marinated in umeboshi vinegar or mixed with mustard and shoyu. Sauerkraut also makes a good filling for greens rolls.

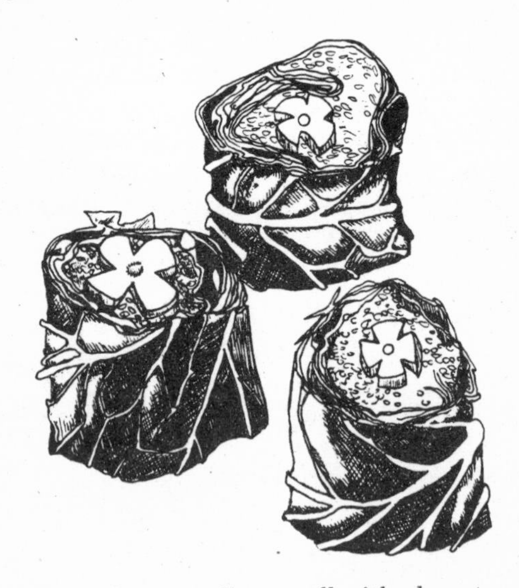

*Serving suggestions:* Greens rolls go well with almost any meal. They are particularly delicious with fish or pressure cooked rice. They go well with *Millet loaf* (see page 59) and make a delightfully light lunch with a *Couscous salad* (see page 66). When attractively arranged on a large plate, greens rolls make delicious party food. When children do not like greens they will almost certainly eat greens rolls if they have plenty of filling in.

# 11. SALADS

There are different types of salads — raw salads, blanched salads, boiled salads and pressed salads. Boiled salads are not commonly used in European or American cuisine but are a delightful addition to the menu in the cooler seasons of the year. A boiled salad consists of three or more vegetables chosen for their complimentary nature and cut into shapes that harmonize well with each other. Emphasis is placed on cutting styles that add sparkle to a meal, such as carrot and radish flowers. Each vegetable is cooked separately for 1 to 3 minutes in boiling water to preserve their different flavours. The vegetable is then placed in a sieve and held under gently running cold water to stop it cooking. The vegetables are then mixed together in an attractive serving bowl.

A dressing should be chosen to harmonize with the rest of the meal. For instance if the rest of the meal is oily, containing burgers or deep-fried foods, then a relatively oil-free salad dressing is a good idea, such as one using umeboshi vinegar or rice vinegar with shoyu or miso.

## BOILED SALADS

### Carrot, Broccoli and Red Radish Boiled Salad

Serves 6.

*6 carrots, 12 radishes, 450 g/1 lb broccoli florettes, 1 pinch sea salt (optional), 150 ml/¼ pt umeboshi vinegar (alternatively 150 ml/¼ pt rice vinegar), 150 ml/¼ pt water*

Wash the carrots, radishes and broccoli florettes. Bring 1 litre/2 pt water to a boil and add the salt if desired. Usually I keep boiled salads salt-free because then they are more refreshing. If a salty taste is required it is preferable to add it in the form of a dressing or sauce. Umeboshi vinegar is a vinegar which has been pickled with sea salt and has a delightful salty and sour flavour.

The carrots can be cut either in matchsticks or into half

moons (see page 42). Cook in boiling water for 2 to 3 minutes, then remove into a sieve and run under cold water to cool. Drain the carrots and place in a serving bowl. Cut the broccoli into florets of the same size and cook for 1 to 2 minutes as for the carrots. Cut the radishes into flowers by cutting down the sides of the radish 4 times to within a ½ cm/¼ inch of the bottom of the radish. Cook for 1 minute, drain and cool.

Mix the carrot and broccoli together in a serving dish. Marinate the radishes in the umeboshi vinegar and water for 1 hour. The radishes go a delightful bright pink on the skins and a more subtle rose colour inside the 'petals'.

After marinating the radishes, prise open the 'petals' if they have not already opened out. Arrange them decoratively over the carrot and broccoli and pour the marinade over the salad immediately before serving. The marinade dressing enhances the deep orange glow of the carrot but tends to discolour the lovely green of the broccoli if put on too long before serving.

*Variations:* Try other dressings on this salad such as *Pumpkin seed dressing* (see page 128) or *Sesame, rice vinegar and umeboshi dressing* (see page 129).

*Serving suggestions:* This salad could be served together with rice and *Seitan strogonoff* (see page 78) or rice and *Aduki, kombu and squash* (see page 85).

## Spring Greens and Sunflower Seed Salad

Serves 6.

*450 g/1 lb spring greens, 340 g/12 oz sunflower seeds, 150 ml/¼ pt umeboshi vinegar, 425 ml/¾ pt water, 1 punnet mustard cress*

Wash and dry roast the sunflower seeds in a frying pan or skillet over a medium heat until they become golden. Stir continuously to prevent burning. Grind 225 g/8 oz of the seeds to a powder in a coffee grinder and mix them with the umeboshi vinegar and water. Let this dressing sit for 30 minutes — this really improves the flavour (add a little ginger juice or mustard for a more piquant flavour).

Wash the spring green leaves, cut out the hard centres and reserve these for making soup stocks. Cut the leaves in half and pile 5 or 6 on top of each other. Cut the leaves into fine diagonal strips.

Bring 1 litre/2 pt water to a boil and add the finely cut spring greens. Cook them for 3 minutes, then run under cold water and transfer to an attractive serving dish.

Pour the dressing over the greens and mix in the remaining roasted sunflower seeds and the mustard cress.

*Variations:* This recipe also works nicely with white cabbage and grated carrot and sesame seeds.

*Serving suggestions:* This salad goes with most grain dishes unless they are very oily. It is also a nice dish to serve with fish.

### Carrot, Leek and Cauliflower Salad with Miso Sauce

Serves 6.

*8 carrots, 2 leeks, 1 cauliflower, 170 g/6 oz pumpkin seeds, 2 tablespoons rice syrup (alternatively use barley malt), 290 ml/½ pt water, 2 tablespoons barley miso*

Bring 1 litre/2 pt water to a boil. Cut the carrots into fine matchsticks and cook in the boiling water for 1 to 2 minutes. Remove into a sieve and run under cold water. Place in a serving dish. Cut the cauliflower into small florets and cook for 1 to 2 minutes as for the carrots. Cut the leeks into thin rounds and also cook as for the carrots. Mix the vegetables together in the serving dish.

Wash and drain the pumpkin seeds. Dry roast on a medium heat, stirring regularly to prevent the seeds burning, until they have all popped. Grind the seeds to a powder in a coffee grinder. Blend the miso in the water. Heat the rice syrup in a pan until it just bubbles and mix in with the miso.

Add the miso and rice syrup to the ground pumpkin seeds and mix them thoroughly to form a creamy dressing. Add more water if necessary to make the desired consistency. Pour the dressing over the salad and serve.

*Variations:* Add a little lemon juice or ginger juice to the dressing to create a more piquant flavour.

### Cabbage and Watercress Salad

Serves 6.

*675 g/1½ lb cabbage, 2 bunches of watercress, 5 tablespoons tahini, 150 ml/¼ pt umeboshi vinegar, 290 ml/½ pt water, 1 tablespoon rice vinegar or lemon juice*

Dice the cabbage into ½ cm/¼ inch squares. Wash the watercress and discard the roots, but keep the stalks where possible. Bring 1 litre/2 pt water to a boil and cook the cabbage for 1 to 2 minutes. Place the cabbage in a sieve and run it gently under cold water until it has cooled. Allow the cabbage to drain. Blanch the watercress very quickly, then cool under cold running water and allow to drain. Cut the watercress into 1 cm/ ½ inch pieces and mix it with the cabbage.

Place the tahini, umeboshi vinegar and water in a suribachi or blender and blend to a smooth creamy consistency. Add the rice vinegar or lemon juice and blend again. Pour this dressing over the salad and garnish with a wedge of lemon or a few sprigs of parsley.

*Serving suggestions:* This dish could be served with a *Cream of carrot and onion soup* (see page 49), *Rice and oats* (see page 55), and *Aduki, kombu and squash* (see page 85).

### Swede Triangle and Almond Salad

Serves 6.

*1 medium swede, 450 g/1 lb brussels sprouts, 170 g/6 oz whole almonds, 150 ml/¼ pt rice vinegar, 2 tablespoons shoyu*

Cut the swede into rectangles 2.5 cm/1 inch square. Cut this square into half diagonally, and cut the resulting triangle into thin triangular slices.

Wash the brussels sprouts and cut them from top to bottom into thin slices. Bring 1 litre/2 pt water to a boil and cook the swede for 1½ minutes. Remove into a sieve and cool under running water, then drain. Then cook the brussels sprouts for 1 minute, cool and drain. Combine the brussels and swede together in a serving bowl.

Dry roast the almonds in a frying pan or under the grill until they turn a light brown colour. Cut each almond down its length into 2 or 3 fine slithers and decorate the salad with them. Mix the shoyu and rice vinegar and pour over the salad no more than 5 minutes before serving, as rice vinegar tends to discolour green vegetables.

*Serving suggestions:* Serve this salad with *Rice croquettes* (see page 56) or *Rice and barley with onions and sesame seeds* (see page 58) and steamed carrots.

## BLANCHED SALADS

### Red Kidney Bean, Celery and Onion Dressed Salad

Serves 6.

*340 g/12 oz cooked red kidney beans, 225 g/8 oz diced celery, 225 g/8 oz diced onion, 340 g/12 oz diced carrots, parsley, chives or spring onions to garnish, 290 ml/½ rice vinegar, 3 tablespoons umeboshi paste, 2 tablespoons water*

Wash and cut the vegetables. Blanch the carrot in 1 litre/2 pt boiling water for 20 to 30 seconds, then cool in a sieve under cold running water and drain. Repeat with the onion and then the celery. Mix the vegetables together in an attractive serving bowl and add the cooked beans. Blend the umeboshi paste in the rice vinegar in a suribachi or blender then mix in the water. Pour over the salad.

Add a little freshly chopped parsley, chives or spring onions for garnish.

*Serving suggestions:* Serve for lunch with *Noodle sushi* (see page 72) or *Couscous loaf* (see page 65). This dish goes down well with a little cucumber or lettuce inside a pitta bread which has been spread with *Tahini shoyu spread* (see page 130).

### Broccoli and Swede Flower Crudités with Carrot and Thyme Dip Sauce

Serves 6.

*450 g/1 lb broccoli, 1 medium swede, 8 carrots, 425 ml/¾ pt water, 170 g/6 oz pumpkin seeds, 2½ tablespoons umeboshi paste or barley miso, 1 teaspoon dried thyme*

Wash and cut the broccoli into large florets, then cut these in half so that there is a smooth edge for scooping up the dip. Cut the swede into a 3½ cm/1½ inch squares. Make the swede flowers by nicking a v-shape from the corners of each square.

Use the broccoli and swede crudités either raw or blanched for a minute in boiling water and then cooled under cold running water. Blanching and then dowsing in cold water brings out the colour and flavour of the vegetables. The broccoli becomes a lovely bright green and the swede a gently glowing orange. Place the crudités decoratively on a platter.

Prepare the dip sauce as described in the *Carrot and thyme dip sauce* recipe on page 142 and place in a bowl in the centre of a large platter or serving dish. Arrange the broccoli and swede flower crudites around the sauce so that people can scoop up the dip with the vegetables.

## PRESSED SALADS

### Red Radish and Cucumber Pressed Salad

Serves 6.

*3 bunches of red radishes, 1 cucumber, 290 ml/½ pt rice vinegar, 3 tablespoons shoyu*

Wash the radishes and cut them into thin slices. Wash the cucumber and dice it. Place the cucumber in a salad press with the radish on top. Mix 150 ml/¼ pt rice vinegar with the shoyu and pour it over the cucumber and red radish. Press the salad for at least 2 hours before serving. This salad can be prepared in the morning for the evening.

If you do not have a salad press, put the cucumber and radish in a bowl and cover with a saucer or plate. Put a heavy weight on top of the plate, such as a large food storage jar or a pan of water.

Squeeze the salad between the hands to remove excess liquid. Place the salad decoratively in a bowl and pour over the remaining rice vinegar.

*Variations:* Rinse and soak 225 g/4 oz dulse or wakame sea vegetable in water to cover until softened. Chop finely and add to pressed cucumber. Dry roasted sunflower seeds, pumpkin seeds or almonds can be mixed with pressed salads. Cut the roasted almonds into thin slithers.

## RAW SALADS

### Carrot and Cucumber Salad

Serves 6.

*8 carrots, 1 cucumber, 6 bright green lettuce leaves, 2½ tablespoons umeboshi paste or vinegar, 2 onions, 2 tablespoons rice vinegar or cider vinegar, 290 ml/½ pt water*

Dice the carrots finely and the cucumber into larger pieces. Wash the lettuce leaves and cover a serving dish with them decoratively. Either mix the cucumber and carrot together and place on the lettuce leaves, or arrange them in alternate strips of orange and pale green around the serving dish.

Dice the onions as finely as possible and purée in a suribashi or blender to a smooth paste. Add the umeboshi and rice vinegar and mix them together well. Add the water and blend thoroughly. Pour this dressing over the salad 1 hour before serving.

*Variations:* This dressing can be made with spring onions instead of onions and used over a salad of blanched onions cut in half moons and red radishes.

*Serving suggestions:* This salad goes excellently with fish such as *Sole marinade* (see page 96). It can also be served for a summer lunch with steamed whole onions and *Rice sushi* (see page 72).

# 12. SEA VEGETABLES

Sea vegetables are an enormously valuable food, being high in minerals. They can be used in a wide variety of dishes, including soups, stews, with beans and vegetables and in salads. Sea vegetables can also be used as a condiment on rice or other grains — *Kombu powder* or *Nori condiment* (see page 137).

### Arame, Sauerkraut and Almonds

Serves 6.

*225 g/8 oz arame, 340 g/12 oz sauerkraut, 225 g/8 oz whole almonds, 1 tablespoon shoyu*

Rinse and drain the arame quickly in a sieve under a tap. Place the arame in a saucepan with water to just cover. Bring the arame to a boil and add the shoyu. Turn the heat low, cover the pot and simmer for 1 hour. Add a little more water as necessary to prevent the arame burning.

Take the sauerkraut, preferably a low-salt variety, chop it finely and spread over the arame. This prevents the sauerkraut discolouring. Simmer for 10 minutes, then remove the lid and cook away any remaining liquid. Mix the arame and sauerkraut together and place attractively on a serving dish with perhaps a few rounds of cucumber to garnish.

Wash and roast the almonds under the grill or in a frying pan until they turn golden. Allow the almonds to cool and chop them lengthways into fine slithers. Garnish the arame with the almonds.

*Variations:* Roasted sesame seeds, sunflower seeds, pumpkin seeds or walnuts can be used instead of almonds as a garnish. Onions can be used instead of sauerkraut but need to be cooked with the arame for 20 minutes instead of 10.

## Watercress and Nori Rolls

Serves 6.

*3 bunches of watercress, 3 sheets of nori, 170 g/6 oz fine carrot matchsticks, 150 ml/¼ pt umeboshi vinegar, 150 ml/¼ pt water*

Bring 570 ml/1 pt water to a rolling boil and blanch the carrots for little under a minute. Remove the carrots, place them in a sieve and dowse them under gently running cold water. Drain the carrots and place them in a bowl. Mix the umeboshi vinegar and water together and pour this marinade over the carrots. Allow the carrots to steep in the marinade for at least 1 hour, then drain and keep the marinade for a salad dressing or dip sauce.

Meanwhile wash the watercress and blanch it. Again run the watercress under cold running water, then drain and set aside on a plate. Separate the individual stems to allow them to drain further before being wrapped in the nori. If the greens are too wet then the nori will tear.

Toast each sheet of nori about 10 cm/4 inches above a gas flame, moving it around so that every part of the nori changes from brown to emerald green. Hold the nori up to the light to see how evenly it has been toasted. If you have an electric stove, hold close to a ring turned up high.

Place a sheet of nori on a sushi mat or an undyed bamboo mat. Spread about one bunch of the watercress in a line across the sheet of nori. Place some of the carrot matchsticks down the centre of the watercress and roll the nori up in the mat, pulling the edge of the mat back so that it doesn't get rolled up inside

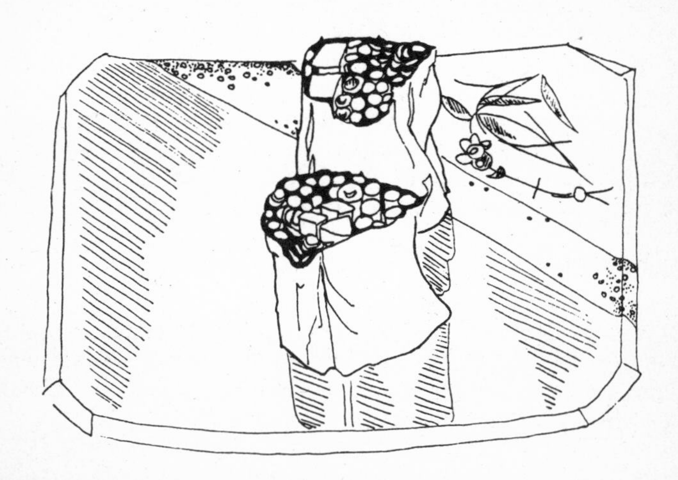

the nori. Roll the nori and vegetables as tightly as possible so that the roll doesn't fall apart. When the nori has been completely rolled up, wrap the sushi mat around the nori roll and squeeze gently but firmly so that the roll sticks together. Unroll the mat and place the roll on a flat dry surface. Use a sharp knife to cut the roll into six equal pieces. Up end each piece to reveal a very attractive and decorative dish. Repeat with the rest of the nori.

*Variations:* Instead of watercress use radish greens, spring greens or kale leaves. The carrot centre can be replaced by red radish matchsticks, sauerkraut, a mustard, shoyu and tahini paste, or a combination of blanched carrot matchsticks and *Pumpkin seed spread* (see page 128).

## Arame, Onions and Dried Daikon

Serves 6.

*170 g/6 oz arame, 6 onions cut in half moons (see page 42), 60 g/2 oz dried daikon, 2 tablespoons shoyu, 1 tablespoon ginger juice (squeezed from freshly grated ginger), parsley to garnish*

Rinse the arame in a sieve under the tap and place in a saucepan with water to cover. Simmer for 30 minutes with a lid. Soak the dried daikon for 5 minutes in water to cover and discard the soaking water. Spread the onions over the arame and then the dried daikon on top. Add water to cover all the ingredients. Do not disturb these layers until the cooking is finished — this layering method of cooking stops the sea vegetable discolouring the other vegetables so that the white of the onion really compliments the brown of the arame.

Cook the arame, onions and dried daikon for 20 minutes, add the shoyu and cook 10 minutes longer. Add the ginger juice and cook for 1 minute. Then serve with a garnish of parsley.

*Serving suggestions:* Serve with *Rice and chestnuts* (see page 56) together with slices of fried seitan and a green salad.

## Arame, Carrot and Sesame Seed Rolls

Serves 6.

*170 g/6 oz arame, 6 carrots, cut in fine matchsticks, 60 g/2 oz sesame seeds, 1 tablespoon shoyu, 225 g/8 oz medium oatflakes, 110 g/4 oz organic pastry flour, 150 ml/¼ pt safflower oil, 1½ teaspoons dried mixed herbs, pinch of sea salt, water to mix to a dough*

Prepare the pastry at least an hour in advance by mixing the oatflakes, flour, herbs and salt together then stir in the oil. The pastry turns out better if it isn't touched too much. Add enough water to make a stiff dough and knead briefly until it makes a ball.

Rinse the arame in a sieve under a tap. Put the arame in a saucepan with water to cover and simmer for 40 minutes. Add a little more water if necessary to prevent burning. Spread the carrot matchsticks over the arame and steam for 10 minutes. Season with the shoyu and cook without a lid until all the liquid has cooked away.

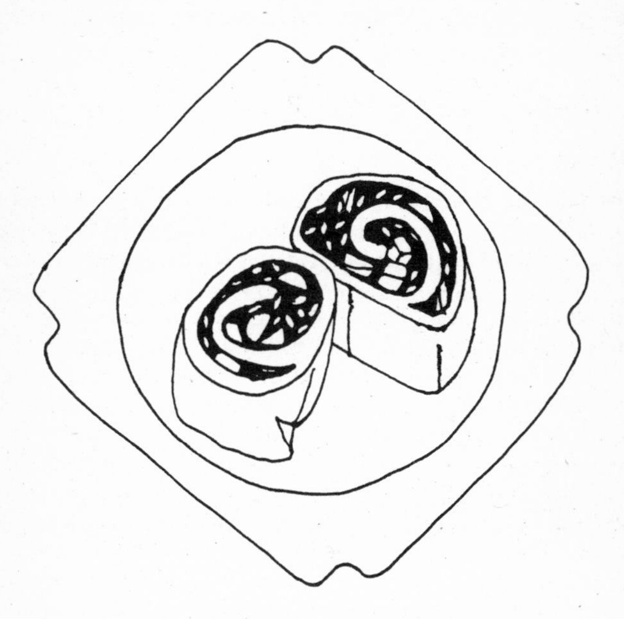

Wash and drain the sesame seeds. Dry roast them on a medium heat for 5-10 minutes until all the seeds have turned golden and easily crush when rubbed between the thumb and third finger. Mix the sesame seeds with the arame and carrot.

Lay the pastry dough between two sheets of greaseproof paper and roll flat. The greaseproof paper enables the pastry to be rolled more thinly. Cut out rectangles about 17 cm by 12 cm/7 inches by 5 inches and place a 5 cm/2 inch wide line of the arame, carrot and sesame seeds filling at one end of each pastry rectangle. Roll the pastry around the filling forming a spiral of pastry and arame filling. Bake these rolls in a preheated oven at 190°C/375°F/Gas Mark 5 for about 25 minutes. Take the rolls out and allow them to cool before cutting them into approximately 2.5 cm/1 inch pieces. Turn the pieces end up to reveal the lovely spiral shape and arrange on a serving dish.

*Serving suggestions:* Serve these rolls as a mid-afternoon or supper snack. They go well with beer. Serve the arame rolls as part of a meal with *Couscous loaf* (see page 65) and a green salad.

## Hiziki, Red Radish and Tofu Salad

Serves 6.

*2 bunches of red radishes, 150 ml/¼ pt umeboshi vinegar (or 2 tablespoons shoyu and 2 tablespoons rice or cider vinegar), 150 ml/¼ pt water, 340 g/12 oz tofu, cut into small cubes, pinch of sea salt, 225 g/8 oz hiziki, 60 g/2 oz sesame seeds, parsley for garnish*

Bring 290 ml/½ pt water to a boil and cook the radishes for 1 minute. Let them cool and then cut into 4 slices. Make up the marinade of umeboshi vinegar and water and steep the red radishes in the marinade for 5 minutes. Remove the radishes and set marinade aside.

Bring another 290 ml/½ pt water to a boil, add a pinch of sea salt and the tofu cubes, and cook for 1 minute. Allow the tofu cubes to cool then pour the marinade over the tofu. Allow the tofu to marinate for at least 2 hours.

Rinse the hiziki in a sieve and place in a saucepan with water to just cover. Simmer for 45 minutes, adding a little more water if necessary. Then remove the lid and cook away any remaining liquid.

Wash the sesame seeds in a sieve and drain them well before dry roasting on a medium heat until golden. Cut the hiziki into 2.5 cm/1 inch lengths and mix it with the radishes and the tofu cubes. Sprinkle the sesame seeds over. Garnish with some finely chopped parsley.

*Variations:* Use cauliflower florets as well as or instead of the red radishes. Cauliflower turns a beautiful delicate pink when marinated in umeboshi vinegar. Carrot matchsticks, cubes and flowers can be used to add a different colour and shape.

## Deep-fried Hiziki Nuggets

Serves 6.

*225 g/8 oz hiziki, 450 g/1 lb tofu, 3 umeboshi plums pitted (or 3 teaspoons umeboshi paste), 1 tablespoon white miso, 1 tablespoon kuzu, 2 teaspoons ginger juice (squeezed from freshly grated ginger), 1 tablespoon rice flour, pastry flour to bind, 3 onions, diced finely, 2 tablespoons very finely chopped parsley, sesame oil for deep-frying, 6 tablespoons grated red radish, 6 drops shoyu*

Rinse the hiziki in a sieve under a tap then place it in a saucepan with water to just cover. Bring to a boil then turn the heat low and cook for 45 minutes. Add a little more water if necessary. At the end of this time remove the lid and cook away any remaining liquid. Remove the hiziki and cut it into 2.5 cm/1 inch lengths.

Place 1 cm/½ inch water and the tofu in a saucepan and steam for 10 minutes. Take the tofu out and blend it to a cream in a suribachi or blender. Purée the umeboshi plums, white miso and kuzu in the minimum of water and mix with the tofu. Add the ginger juice. Mix in the rice flour and enough pastry flour to make the tofu firm and sticky. Mix in the hiziki, chopped parsley and diced onion.

Grate the radishes, add the shoyu, and leave this condiment to stand on one side while deep-frying the nuggets. This is a good condiment to serve with deep-fried foods as it aids the digestion of oily foods.

Wet your hands and roll the hiziki and tofu mixture into balls. Add oil to a depth of 5 cm/2 inches in a saucepan and heat. The oil is hot enough for deep-frying when a small piece of vegetable dropped into the oil quickly rises sizzling to the surface. Cook 2 or 3 nuggets at a time for 3 minutes or so until golden. Remove onto kitchen paper to drain. Serve immediately with a tablespoon of grated red radish condiment per person.

*Variations:* Other sea vegetables such as arame, dulse and kombu can also be used in making these deep-fried nuggets.

# 13. SAUCES AND DRESSINGS

Sauces and dressings can really transform an otherwise simple meal. From children who don't like greens to adults who love rich creamy sauces, there is always a sauce or dressing piquant enough to stimulate the appetite and attractive enough to enhance the decorative appeal of a meal.

## Pumpkin Seed Spread or Dressing

Serves 6.

*225 g/8 oz pumpkin seeds (or sunflower seeds), 2 tablespoons umeboshi paste (or barley miso), 1 teaspoon ginger juice (squeezed from freshly grated ginger), 290 ml/½ pt water*

Wash and drain the pumpkin seeds. Heat a cast iron skillet and add the pumpkin seeds, stir frequently until the seeds pop and turn golden. Grind the seeds to a powder in a coffee grinder or suribachi to obtain a nuttier texture.

Mix the umeboshi paste with 2 tablespoons of the water to a smooth cream in a suribachi or bowl. Add the rest of the water and then slowly fold in the pumpkin seeds. Mix in the ginger juice and allow to sit for a few minutes before serving.

Another 290 ml/½ pt water can be added to turn this spread into a dressing for salads and grains.

*Variations:* There are endless delicious variations on this recipe. Try pumpkin seeds, umeboshi vinegar and a dash of mustard, or pumpkin seeds, barley miso and a little lemon juice. Sesame seeds are lovely with white miso and ginger juice. A little mustard cress or finely chopped parsley can be added to give extra colour and taste.

*Serving suggestions:* Serve the spread with crackers, *Millet loaf* (see page 59) or *Couscous loaf* (see page 65).

## Peanut Sauce

Serves 6.

*110 g/4 oz red skinned peanuts, 720 ml/1¼ pt water, 3 tablespoons kuzu, 2 tablespoons barley miso, 4 teaspoons ginger juice (squeezed from freshly grated ginger)*

Dry roast the peanuts in a skillet or under the grill until they turn a golden colour. Grind them to a powder in a coffee grinder. Blend the miso with just enough water to mix it to a paste. Bring the 720 ml/1¼ pt water to a boil, add the miso and simmer on a very low heat for 3 minutes.

Add the ground peanuts and stir them in well with the liquid. Blend the kuzu in 4 or 5 tablespoons of cold water, take the sauce off the heat and stir in the kuzu. Replace the sauce on a low heat and stir it until it thickens. Add the ginger juice, turn off the heat and serve the sauce immediately.

*Variations:* You can use sesame seeds, sunflower seeds, or almonds instead of the peanuts, and umeboshi vinegar instead of ginger.

*Serving suggestions:* Serve over fried seitan, *Millet loaf* (see page 59), *Millet and lentil burgers* (see page 60), or over a salad of grated carrot and finely cut spring onions.

## Sesame, Rice Vinegar and Umeboshi Dressing

Serves 6.

*225 g/8 oz sesame seeds or 6 tablespoons dark tahini, 290 ml /½ pt rice vinegar, 570 ml/1 pt water, 3 tablespoons umeboshi paste (or white miso)*

Wash and drain the sesame seeds. Dry roast them in a frying pan or skillet on a medium heat, stirring them constantly for about 5 minutes. Cook until they become golden and crush easily when rubbed gently between the thumb and third finger.

Grind the seeds in a coffee grinder or suribachi until at least two-thirds are ground to a powder. Shake the umeboshi paste in a jar with 290 ml/½ pt of the water until there are no lumps left. Pour the water and umeboshi over the ground sesame seeds and blend them in the suribachi or bowl to a paste. Mix in the remaining water and the rice vinegar to make the dressing.

*Serving suggestions:* This dressing is particularly nice over boiled salads such as leek boiled salad or *Carrot, broccoli and red radish boiled salad* (see page 115).

## Ginger Shoyu Dip Sauce

Serves 6.

*290 ml/½ pt shoyu, 290 ml/½ pt water, 150 ml/¼ pt ginger juice (squeezed from freshly grated ginger)*

Prepare the ginger juice by washing the fresh ginger root, grating it and squeezing out the juice. When you have squeezed the pulp of the ginger dry, wet it with a little water and squeeze the juice out again. Mix the ginger, shoyu and water together. Place it in two or more attractive dipping bowls and allow it to sit for a few minutes before serving.

*Serving suggestions:* Serve with deep-fried foods such as *Deep-fried stuffed seitan* (see page 79), *Tempuru vegetables* (see page 108), or deep-fried grain balls such as *Rice croquettes* (see page 56) or *Deep-fried millet balls* (see page 62).

## Mustard Shoyu Dip Sauce

Serves 6.

*290 ml/½ pt shoyu, 2 tablespoons ready made mustard, 290 ml/½ pt water, 2 tablespoons rice vinegar (optional)*

Blend the mustard and shoyu in a suribachi or bowl. Add the water slowly, blending it as you go. For a more sparkling flavour also add the rice vinegar. Place in 2 or 3 individual dipping bowls and leave to sit for a few minutes before serving.

*Serving suggestions:* Serve with deep-fried grain balls or fish, particularly flat fish such as plaice, turbot or brill.

## Tahini Shoyu Spread or Dressing

Serves 6.

*12 tablespoons tahini, 3 tablespoons shoyu, 5 to 6 spring onions, 1 tablespoons umeboshi vinegar, 150 ml/¼ pt water*

Blend the tahini, shoyu and water in a suribachi or blender, mix in the umeboshi vinegar and let the spread sit while you wash and cut the spring onions finely on the diagonal. Mix the spring onions into the spread and serve.

To make into a dressing, add water until you reach the desired consistency.

*Serving suggestions:* Use this spread on *Millet loaf* (see page 59) or on crackers. Or use as the basis of stuffed pita breads with a *Split pea pâté* (see page 88) or *Lentil pâté* (see page 85) and some salad. As a dressing it is lovely over a raw lettuce and cucumber salad or a boiled salad of carrot and cauliflower.

## Mustard Miso Dressing

Serves 6.

*570 ml/1 pt water, 5 tablespoons barley miso, 2 tablespoons ready-made mustard, 1½ teaspoons ginger juice (squeezed from freshly grated ginger)*

Blend the miso to a paste with a little of the water in a suribachi or bowl, then blend in the mustard. Mix in the rest of the water and the ginger juice.

*Serving suggestions:* Serve over *Deep-fried stuffed seitan* (see page 79), *Deep-fried tempeh* (see page 80) or any boiled or raw salad.

# 14. PICKLES, GARNISHES AND CONDIMENTS

## PICKLES

### Brine Pickles

*900 g/2 lb carrots, onions, radishes, red cabbage, greens stalks, or cauliflower, 1 teaspoon sea salt, 570 ml/1 pt water*

Cut several of the above vegetables into attractive shapes (see Chapter 9). Include some onion as it enhances the sour tang of all the pickled vegetables. Pack the vegetables tightly in a glass jar or ceramic pot, leaving a little space at the top.

Make the pickling brine by boiling up the salt in the water until it dissolves. Let the brine cool to hand temperature, and pour over the vegetables. Weigh the vegetables down with a stone or other heavy object so that they remain beneath the level of the brine.

Cover the jar with cheesecloth and put it in a warm place. The vegetables take from 3 days to 3 weeks to ferment and pickle, depending on the temperature. Taste a piece of vegetable every few days. When it no longer tastes raw but has a sour flavour the pickles are done. If the pickles are left too long they may develop a mouldy flavour. When they have finished pickling, keep in the refrigerator and use over the next 2 or 3 weeks.

*Variations:* Adding a few squares of red cabbage turns the pickling juice red and all the vegetables become a different shade of pink. The radishes become pinky red, the carrots orange rose, and the cauliflower pale pink. These pickles look beautiful in a small white serving dish.

*Serving suggestions:* Pickles can be used as garnishes to decorate dishes and as a filling for *Noodle sushi* (see page 72) if they have been cut into long matchsticks. They are excellent served with oily or heavy foods such as fish and deep-fried foods.

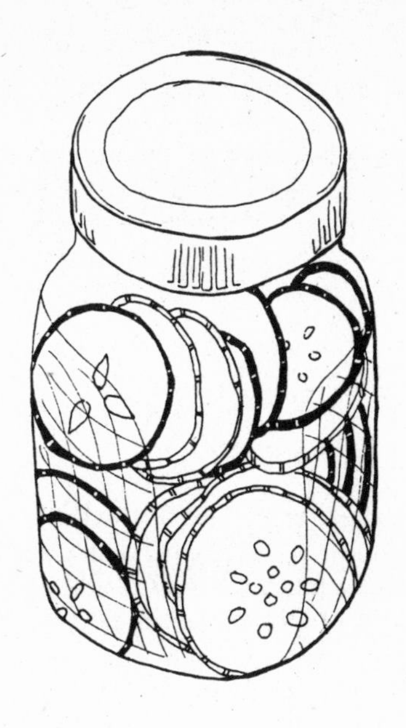

## Onion Miso Quick Pickles

*3 or 4 onions, cut in very fine half moons (see page 42), 3 tablespoons barley miso, 3 tablespoons water*

Place the cut onions in a salad press or bowl. Blend the miso in the water and mix this evenly through the onions. Press the onions for at least 2 hours in the salad press or, if you are using a bowl, with a saucer on the onions weighed down with a heavy storage jar or pot of water. It can be left pressing for a day or two to produce a stronger tasting pickle.

## Red Radishes in Umeboshi Vinegar

*1 bunch red radishes, 290 ml/½ pt umeboshi vinegar, 290 ml/ ½ pt water*

Bring 570 ml/1 pt water to a boil. Wash the whole radishes and nip the root tails off. Leave any green shoots on. Blanch the radishes in the boiling water for 30 seconds, then remove and place them in a sieve. Put the sieve under gently running cold water for 1 to 2 minutes, then drain.

Mix the umeboshi vinegar and water to make a pickling juice. Put the radishes in a bowl and pour this over them. Leave the radishes at least 1 hour, but preferably 2 to 4 hours before serving.

*Serving suggestions:* Serve them as they are or cut them decoratively into *Radish flowers* (see page 135). After pickling, the whole radishes can be sliced finely and mixed with a green salad or *Rice salad* (see page 57) or laid attractively on fish as a garnish.

### Green Beans and Carrot Matchsticks in Shoyu and Ginger

*110 g/4 oz green beans, 225 g/8 oz carrots, cut into long medium sized matchsticks, 150 ml/¼ pt shoyu, 720 ml/1¼ pt water, 4 cm/1½ inch piece fresh ginger root*

Place the fresh, washed ginger root at the bottom of a jar. If necessary head and tail the beans, then mix with the carrot matchsticks and pack tightly on top of the ginger. Mix the shoyu and water together and pour it into the jar to cover the vegetables.

Place a stone or other small heavy object on the vegetables to keep them beneath the shoyu pickling liquid. Cover the pickles with cheesecloth and store in a warm place. They will take from 4 days to 3 weeks to pickle, depending on the temperature. Taste a piece of bean or carrot every few days — when they have lost their rawness and developed a sour taste, put them in a refrigerator. Here they will last for 2 or 3 weeks.

*Serving suggestions:* Have a few pickles with your meals every day — they add a delightful taste and texture to any meal. They are delicious served in the centre of *Noodle sushi* (see page 72), *Greens rolls* (see page 113), or *Watercress and nori rolls* (see page 123).

## GARNISHES

Garnishes can be anything from a sprig of parsley or a twist of lemon to an elaborately cut piece of carrot or cucumber. They can take anything from a few seconds to five minutes to prepare and the simplest of garnishes are often the most attractive.

## Gherkin Fans

Gherkin fans are very attractive. The same fans can also be made using dwarf cucumbers or long oval-shaped red radishes. Take the gherkin and cut parallel slits down two-thirds the length of it, moving towards the root end. Spread the fan out and press the joined end with a spoon to make the fan spread out.

This fan is very attractive as a garnish for large-scale presentations of food at dinners and parties.

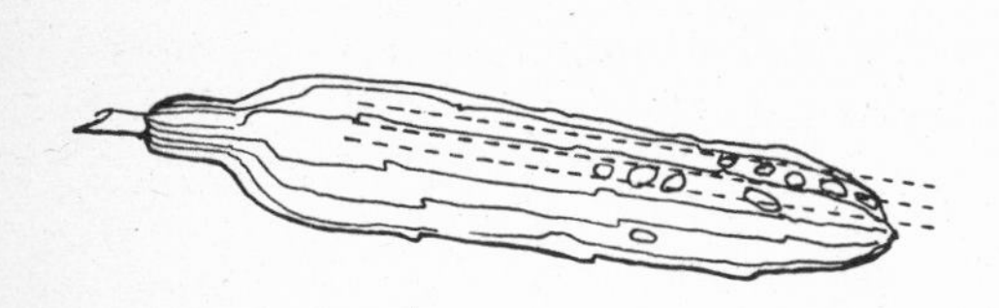

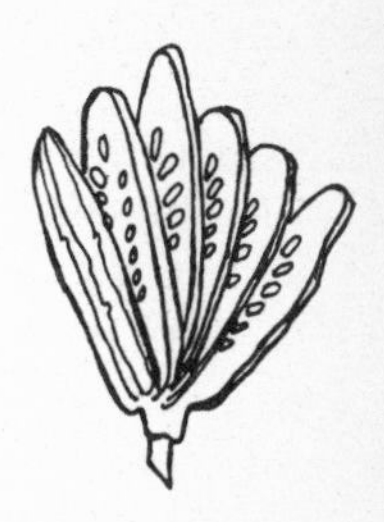

## Radish Flowers

The simplest kind of radish flower has four petals, made by cutting 4 slits down each side of a radish. They can be set to garnish a bowl of greens or a *Rice salad* (see page 57). If radish flowers are marinated in 50 per cent umeboshi vinegar and 50 per cent rice vinegar they turn a very bright pinky red, which is extremely beautiful and appetizing to look at.

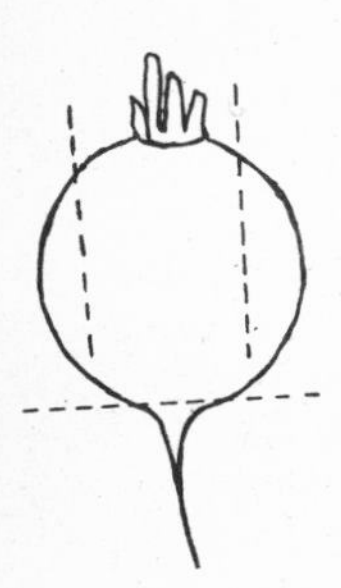

## Lemon Rings

Lemon rings are another pretty garnish, particularly suited to fish and desserts. Cut thin slices of lemon. Cut out the flesh of half the lemon slice, leaving the rind intact. Make one cut through the rind where the lemon flesh ends, and curl the rind delicately over the half with the flesh left.

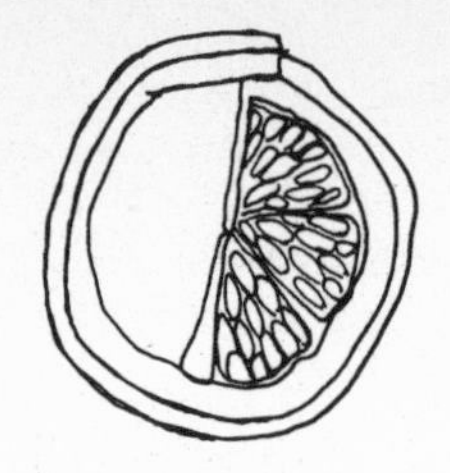
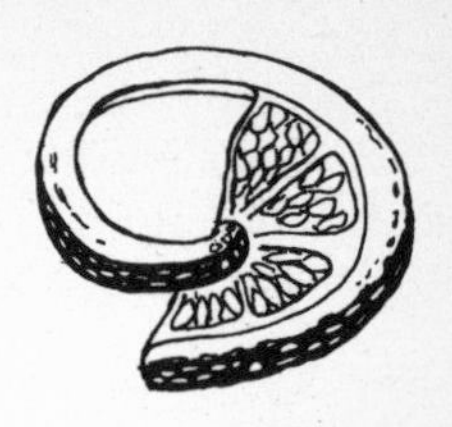

**Spring Onion Feathers**
Cut the top two-thirds off a spring onion. Remove the roots but keep the white part of the spring onion bulb. Cut very thin slithers into the spring onion as far down as the beginning of the white part of the onion bulb. If delicately done the spring onion leaves can then be parted and spread out to look like feathers or a fan. This garnish can be used for almost any dish — they look pretty laid on top of a *Rice croquette* (see page 56) or *Couscous rissole* (see page 66) or on top of a whole fillet of fish.

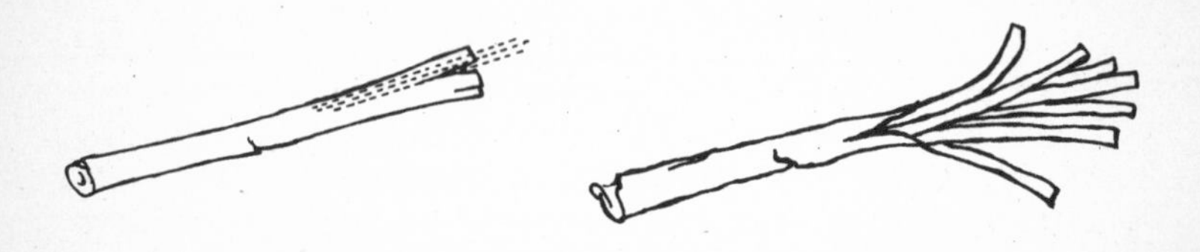

CONDIMENTS

**Gomasio**

*110 g/4 oz unhulled sesame seeds, 1 teaspoon sea salt*

The quantities of ingredients can be doubled or trebled to make a larger amount of condiment. Wash and drain the sesame seeds. Place them in a dry frying pan or skillet and roast on a medium heat, stirring continuously until the seeds become golden and crush easily when rubbed gently between the thumb and third finger. Place the seeds in a bowl to cool. Wipe out the skillet, add the salt, and roast for a few minutes. Place the salt in a suribachi and grind to a fine powder.

Put the sesame seeds in the suribachi and grind until half of them are ground, and the seeds are well mixed with the salt. Place the finished gomasio in a jar and use ½ to 1 teaspoon a day as a condiment on rice, noodles, and other grain dishes.

Gomasio can be used as a seasoning in *Rice croquettes* (see page 56) or in salad dressings, but is too salty for small children. For children use roasted and ground sesame seeds mixed with green nori flakes.

## Nori Condiment

*3 sheets of nori sea vegetable, 190 ml/⅓ pt water, 1 teaspoon ginger juice (squeezed from freshly grated ginger)*

Tear the nori sheets up into very small pieces. Pour the water into a heavy cast iron skillet and put the nori pieces into the water. Let the nori soak in the water for 6 to 8 minutes, then put the skillet on a medium heat. After 6 to 7 minutes the nori condiment should be becoming quite dry. Add the ginger juice, cook until the nori becomes a thick paste, and serve with rice or another grain.

## Kombu Powder

*3 × 15 cm/6 inch strips of kombu*

Heat the oven for 10 to 20 minutes at 190°C/375°F/Gas Mark 5. Place the kombu strips on a baking tray and bake them for about 45 minutes until the kombu is crisp and can be broken up between the fingers. Break the kombu into little pieces into a suribachi and grind to a powder. If some pieces refuse to break up, put them back in the oven to dry out more. Store in a jar and use 1 to 2 teaspoons a day.

*Variations:* The same procedure can be followed with wakame or dulse. These sea vegetables will bake more quickly — on average in about 20 minutes. To make a different kind of condiment, mix the sea vegetable powder with roasted and ground sesame seeds in the proportions of 1:4.

For a sweeter taste, particularly for children, when the seeds have finished dry roasting sprinkle apple juice over them. Continue roasting until the seeds re-crispen, then mix the seeds with the powdered sea vegetable.

*Serving suggestions:* Use these condiments over porridge instead of salt, and on almost any grain or vegetable dish. They have lovely flavours and are very rich in minerals.

## Sesame Shiso Leaf Condiment

*225 g/8 oz shiso leaves, 225 g/8 oz sesame seeds*

Shiso leaves come together with umeboshi plums. This condiment is a good way of using up these shiso leaves.

Spread the shiso leaves out on a baking tray and bake at 190°C/375°F/Gas Mark 5 for 10 to 20 minutes until they are crisp and completely dried out. Then crush them to a powder in a suribachi and place in a bowl.

Wash and dry roast the sesame seeds until they turn golden and easily crush between the thumb and third finger. Grind the seeds in a suribachi until about half are powdered, then place them in a bowl. Mix the seeds and shiso leaves in the proportion of 1 part shiso leaf to 4 parts sesame seeds and store in a jar. Use one or more teaspoonfuls a day.

*Variations:* Powdered shiso leaves can also be bought in packets and can be used in this form to make this condiment. Pumpkin seeds can be used instead of sesame seeds for a richer, more zestful condiment.

Baked and powdered shiso leaves make a delicious condiment on their own over all kinds of rice and vegetable dishes. They can also be used to make the flavour of salad dressings more piquant.

*Serving suggestions:* Sesame shiso leaf condiment can be mixed with a little rice vinegar and water to make a dressing for salads, a garnish for fish dishes or a seasoning over breakfast porridge.

## Corn Relish

*2 cobs of corn, ½ small green pepper, finely diced, 2 onions, finely diced, 1½ umeboshi plums, 3 tablespoons rice vinegar, 1 tablespoon sesame oil, 1 tablespoon rice syrup or barley malt, 60 g/2 oz chives, spring onions or parsley, finely chopped*

Cut the corn from the cob by cutting down the length of the cob, rotating the cob through 60 degrees, and then repeating the cutting action. Do this 5 times.

Heat the sesame oil in a skillet or frying pan and add the green pepper. Sauté for 7 minutes, stirring frequently, preferably with chopsticks. Chopsticks turn the vegetables over without breaking them up. Add the diced onion and sauté until it becomes transparent. Add the corn and sauté until it becomes golden. Blend the umeboshi in the rice vinegar in a suribachi, add to the pan and cook for 2 minutes on a low heat. Mix in the rice syrup or malt so that it melts but does not burn. Take the corn relish off the heat and add the chopped chives, spring onions or parsley.

*Serving suggestions:* Serve this relish as a condiment with grilled or boiled white fish. If fish has been deep-fried the oil in the fish will tend to make the corn relish taste less good. Corn relish is also good with chicken.

# 15. SNACKS

Snacks often consist of bread with some sort of spread, usually animal quality in nature. Many breads however are heavy and indigestible, making us slower and more sluggish. Pitta bread is a very good and tasty substitute for ordinary bread, being lighter and more digestible. Crackers are also excellent for snacks — try water biscuits, rye crackers, rice crackers or matzos. Here is a recipe for oatflake biscuits and some ideas for spreads and dips to accompany them and the various other breads and crackers.

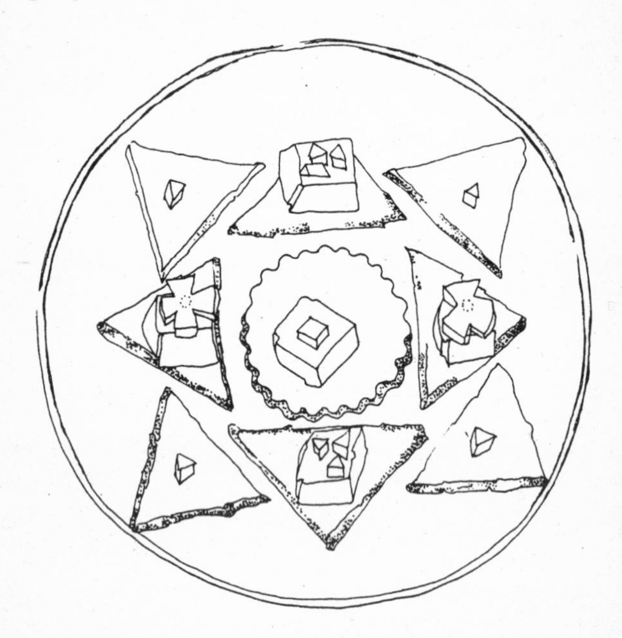

## Oatflake Biscuits

*340 g/12 oz medium oatflakes, 170 g/6 oz pastry flour, 150 ml /¼ pt safflower, sesame or corn oil, 1 pinch sea salt, water to mix (or vegetable stock)*

Mix the oats, flour and salt together, then rub in the oil. Add enough water to mix it to a stiff dough. Roll out between greaseproof paper to about ½ cm/¼ inch thick. Cut the biscuits with a crinkled round pastry cutter and cook in a pre-heated oven at 180°C/350°F/Gas Mark 4 for 15 to 20 minutes until they become golden but not brown. Check the biscuits regularly because if they are overdone they become very hard and unpleasant to eat.

*Serving suggestions:* These savoury biscuits are delicious by themselves or can be spread with any of the following spreads and dips.

## Cucumber, White Miso and Tahini Spread

*1½ cucumbers, sliced finely, 2 tablespoons white miso, 1 tablespoon tahini, lemon juice or ginger juice to taste*

Blend all the ingredients except the lemon or ginger juice together in a liquidizer, then place in a frying pan or skillet and gently simmer for 10 minutes or until it is thick enough to serve as a spread. Add a little lemon juice or ginger juice and put into a serving dish.

*Variations:* Cook with a little thyme instead of ginger, or a garnish of green nori flakes or finely chopped parsley.

## Sunset Dip

*6 large carrots, finely grated, 2 tablespoons white miso, 1 tablespoon ginger juice (squeezed from freshly grated ginger), 2 tablespoons umeboshi vinegar, 4 cloves garlic, finely chopped, 3 tablespoons finely chopped chives (or 3 to 4 spring onions), 4 tablespoons sunflower spread*

Dry roast the grated carrot in a cast iron skillet or frying pan for 4 to 5 minutes. Add a little water and cook for another 10 minutes. Allow any liquid to cook away and place all the ingredients, except the chives, together in a blender. Blend until a golden cream is formed. If the cream is too runny, gently simmer it in a frying pan until it is thick enough to make a pleasant dip. Place in an attractive serving dish and garnish with the chives.

*Serving suggestions:* This dip is delicious served with crackers or plain corn chips.

## Onion Butter

For the basic recipe see page 98 in Chapter 14. Onion butter is delicious on bread and crackers and can be livened up with a little ginger juice and some mustard cress.

*Variations:* Pumpkin butter, made in the same way as onion butter, can be a delicious, seasonal alternative.

## Houmous

Recipes for houmous abound. Basically it is a combination of cooked chick peas blended with tahini, lemon juice and salt. Umeboshi paste used instead of salt adds a nice tang. Add a little garlic and the dish is complete. A lot of people find that houmous substitutes for cheese cravings.

## Carrot and Thyme Dip Sauce

*8 carrots, grated finely, 425 ml/¾ pt water, 170 g/6 oz pumpkin seeds, 2½ tablespoons umeboshi paste or barley miso, 1½ teaspoons dried thyme*

Bring 150 ml/¼ pt water to a simmer in a cast iron frying pan or skillet. Add the grated carrot and water sauté for 8 to 10 minutes on a medium heat until it is soft and sweet.

Dry roast the pumpkin seeds in a frying pan on a medium heat until they all pop and have turned golden. Grind the pumpkin seeds to a powder in a coffee grinder. Blend the umeboshi paste in the rest of the water and mix with the ground seeds. Add to the carrots and sauté on a gentle heat until the dip thickens. Add the thyme, turn off the heat and cover with a lid. Let the thyme gently blend with the other flavours in the dip for at least half an hour before serving.

## Tofu Spread

*15 cm/6 inch strip of kombu, 450 g/1 lb firm tofu, 3 tablespoons barley miso, 2 cloves garlic, chopped very finely, ½ cucumber, finely diced, 170 g/6 oz sunflower seeds, 2 tablespoons umeboshi vinegar or shoyu*

Place the kombu in a saucepan with a 1 cm/½ inch of water and the tofu. Steam for 10 minutes and then blend with the tofu, miso, garlic and diced cucumber to a fine cream in a suribachi or blender.

Wash and dry roast the sunflower seeds until they turn golden. Sprinkle the umeboshi vinegar (it has a far more subtle and more piquant taste than shoyu) over the seeds and cook over a gentle heat for one more minute so that they crispen again. Sprinkle these over the tofu spread.

*Serving suggestions:* Tofu spread is a delicious filling for grilled or steamed pitta breads or can be used in sandwiches and on crackers.

## Carrot and Sesame Spread

*8 large carrots grated, 225 g/8 oz sesame seeds, 2 tablespoons umeboshi paste, 2 punnets of mustard cress, 425 ml/¾ pt water*

Heat 150 ml/¼ pt water in a skillet or frying pan. Add the grated carrot and water sauté for 10 minutes. Wash the sesame seeds and roast in a frying pan until golden. Grind to a powder in a coffee grinder or suribachi. Add the ground seeds to the carrots. Blend the umeboshi paste with the remaining water, add to the carrot and seeds and cook for a few minutes until the spread thickens. Blend this mixture to a cream with half the mustard cress in a blender. Serve with the other half of the mustard cress as a garnish.

*Variations:* For a variation use finely diced onion instead of carrot and blend with tahini and umeboshi vinegar.

*Serving suggestions:* Fill grilled or steamed pitta breads with this creamy spread. Use the onion cream version in a pitta bread with a thin slice of smoked tofu and a generous garnish of mustard cress or a piece of lettuce.

# 16. DESSERTS

Unfortunately most desserts are heaped with refined sugar and dairy products. However it is really not necessary to use these to produce sweet and tempting desserts. For sweetness you can use less refined forms of sugar like barley malt and rice syrup. These are made by fermenting grains to break the starch of the grain down into simple sugars. Also try another form of sugar known as *amasake*, again made by fermenting rice or other grains. It is delicious and children love it.

### Apple and Raisin Crumble

Serves 6.

*6 large eating apples, 170 g/6 oz raisins, 860 ml/1½ pt water, 2 tablespoons kuzu, 225 g/8 oz medium oatflakes, 4 tablespoons barley malt, 60 g/2 oz sunflower seeds, 90 g/3 oz sesame seeds, 2 tablespoons safflower or sunflower oil, 1 pinch of sea salt (optional)*

Wash the apples, cut into quarters and remove the cores. Then cut into thin half moons and place in a bowl for use later. Bring to a rolling boil 425 ml/¾ pt water, add the washed raisins and stir gently until the raisins separate and come to the surface. Cover the saucepan and allow the raisins to cook until all the water has been absorbed. Add the rest of the water, bring it to a boil again, then take the pan off the heat. Mix the kuzu with 2 to 3 tablespoons of cold water and stir into the raisins. Place the pan back on a low heat for 1 or 2 minutes, stirring until the kuzu has thickened. Add the apple pieces and cover them with the hot kuzu sauce to blanch them. Pour the apple and raisin mixture into an attractive ovenproof dish.

Wash the sesame seeds and roast in a frying pan until they turn golden. Then grind to a powder in a suribachi or coffee grinder. Mix the oatflakes and ground sesame seeds together. Add the sea salt if you feel the need and then blend in the oil. Heat the barley malt for 1 or 2 minutes on a low heat until it is runny and stir the malt into the oat and sesame seed mixture.

Add the sunflower seeds and then spread the mixture over the apple and raisins. Bake for 30 to 40 minutes at 180°C/350°F/Gas Mark 4.

## Chestnut and Amasake Kuzu

Serves 6.

*450 g/1 lb short grain brown rice or sweet rice, 1 litre/2 pt water, 2 drops shoyu, 190 ml/⅓ pt white rice koji, 110 g/4 oz dried chestnuts, 1 pinch sea salt or 1 teaspoon shoyu, 1 tablespoon kuzu*

Wash the rice and boil with the water and shoyu for 40 minutes. Transfer the rice to a pan or dish that can go in the oven and on a gas or electric ring. Allow the rice to cool until you can put 3 fingers deep into it and hold them there for the count of five. Mix the rice koji thoroughly with the rice. Place the pan or dish in the oven at the lowest setting for 4 to 8 hours or overnight. The rice should be kept at hand temperature — do not let it get any hotter or the fermenting organisms in the koji will be killed and will not produce *amasake.*

Koji is white rice covered in *Aspergillus* spores that break the starch in the rice down into simple sugars. The rice becomes very sweet and delicious. If the koji is left too long in the oven, the rice becomes sweet and sour which adults often like, but both children and adults tend to prefer sweet-tasting amasake. Taste the amasake every hour or so to see if it has developed a sweet taste. When it is ready remove from the oven. Simmer the amasake for 5 minutes to kill the spores and make the amasake sweeter. Blend the amasake to a cream in a blender.

While the amasake is fermenting, soak the chestnuts for 4 to 8 hours or overnight, in enough water to cover. Place the soaked chestnuts in a pressure cooker with their soaking water and the sea salt or shoyu. Add 720 ml/1¼ pt water and pressure cook for 35 minutes. Alternatively boil for 1 hour with a little more water. Bring the pressure down and purée the chestnuts in a suribachi or blender.

Blend the kuzu in a little cold water and reheat the amasake. Take the amasake off the heat, add the kuzu and the puréed chestnuts, then heat until it thickens, stirring constantly. Serve with a garnish of lemon rind and flaked almonds.

*Serving suggestions:* This is a delicious dish for parties and evening suppers. Amasake is popular because it is a ready substitute for custard and is sugar-free. The puréed amasake can be used without the chestnuts as a sauce for *Apple and raisin crumble* (see page 144), Christmas pudding, mince pies

and cakes. You can also buy several different makes of prepared amasake.

### Apple Couscous Cake

Serves 6.

*5 sweet red eating apples, 1 litre/2 pt fresh apple juice, 1½ tablespoons agar agar flakes, 2 tablespoons kuzu, 425 ml/ ¾ pt barley malt, rind of 1 lemon, 1 teaspoon vanilla extract, 340 g/ 12 oz refined couscous, 1 pinch sea salt, 170 g/6 oz nibbed almonds (or sunflower seeds)*

Use a cake tin with a removable base as this is an upside-down cake. Wash the apples, cut into quarters and remove the cores. Cut into thin half moons and spread them out in the bottom of the cake tin half overlapping each other.

Heat 290 ml/½ pt apple juice and 290 ml/½ pt water with the agar agar flakes and cook for 15 minutes. Dilute the kuzu with 2 to 3 tablespoons of cold water. Remove the apple juice from the heat, add the kuzu and cook for 2 minutes stirring constantly while it thickens. Add 2 tablespoons barley malt and cook for 2 minutes more. Pour this sauce over the apples.

Heat the rest of the apple juice with 290 ml/½ pt water. Stir in the remaining barley malt, the lemon rind and vanilla extract. Pour in the couscous and replace the lid immediately. Leave on a low heat, preferably with a flame tamer underneath, for 4 to 5 minutes. Turn the heat off and allow the couscous to carry on cooking for 10 minutes with the lid on. Dry roast the nibbed almonds in a skillet or frying pan and mix them into the couscous, keeping a few aside for a garnish.

Spoon the couscous cake mixture on top of the apples and sauce in the cake tin and press down firmly. Leave 2 to 3 hours to cool before turning the cake out gently onto a plate. Garnish with the remaining nibbed almonds.

*Serving suggestions:* Serve for afternoon tea or as a dessert with some amasake (see *Chestnut and amasake kuzu* recipe on page 145).

## Dandelion Coffee Mousse with Sesame Cream

Serves 6.

*1 litre/2 pt water, 4 tablespoons dandelion root coffee, 4 tablespoons agar agar flakes, 4½ tablespoons kuzu, 6 tablespoons barley malt, 225 g/8 oz sesame seeds, 425 ml/ ¾ pt water, 3 tablespoons rice syrup, 60 g/2 oz flaked almonds*

To make the mousse, bring the water to a boil and add the dandelion coffee. Simmer for 10 minutes then remove the roots by pouring the coffee through a sieve into another saucepan. Save the dandelion roots for reuse (it makes a lovely drink with barley malt). Add the agar agar flakes and simmer for 10 to 15 minutes until they have completely dissolved.

Mix 2 tablespoons kuzu with 2 to 3 tablespoons of cold water. Remove the dandelion coffee from the heat and stir in the kuzu. Return the pan to a gentle heat and stir until it thickens. Add the barley malt, cook for 2 minutes more and then pour into a pyrex dish to cool. When the mousse is half set after about 1 hour, blend it in a blender to a creamy consistency. Half fill individual serving dishes or glasses with the mousse.

To make the sesame cream, wash and dry roast the sesame seeds until they crush easily when rubbed between the thumb and third finger. Put the seeds in a coffee grinder and blend them to a powder.

Bring the 425 ml/¾ pt water to a simmer, add the sesame seeds and cook for 5 minutes. Blend the remaining 2½ tablespoons kuzu with a little cold water, take the saucepan off the heat and stir in the kuzu. Replace the pan on the heat and stir until the mixture thickens. Add the rice syrup and cook 1 minute more. Blend the sesame cream again for a smoother consistency, and pour it over the dandelion coffee mousse. Garnish with a few flaked almonds.

*Serving suggestions:* This dessert can look really beautiful if it is served carefully in delicate bowls with either a light coloured garnish (the almonds) on the dark ground of the dandelion kuzu, or a dark coloured garnish (roasted hazelnuts) on the light coloured ground of the sesame cream.

## Bulghur and Sunflower Seed Cake

Serves 6.

*340 g/12 oz fine bulghur wheat, 1¼ litres/2¼ pt water, 225 g/ 8 oz raisins, 3 tablespoons barley malt, 170 g/6 oz sunflower seeds, 2 pinches sea salt*

Rinse the bulghur wheat in a sieve and leave it to soak in 290 ml/½ pt of the water. Simmer the raisins in another 290 ml/ ½ pt of the water with a lid until all the water has been absorbed. Add the remaining 720 ml/1¼ pt water and bring to a boil. Add the bulghur wheat and salt, turn the heat very low and using a flame tamer if you have one, simmer the bulghur for 20 minutes. Mix in the barley malt and simmer for a further 1 minute.

Meanwhile wash and drain the sunflower seeds and dry roast in a frying pan until they are golden. Stir them frequently or they will be burn. Blend the sunflower seeds to a powder in a coffee grinder and mix them in with the bulghur wheat. The mixture should now be fairly stiff — if it isn't cook the mixture gently with the lid off for as much as 10 minutes more. Turn the mixture into a round mould, press it down firmly, and chill for 1 to 2 hours until it is set. Then carefully turn out onto a serving plate.

*Serving suggestions:* Serve the cake with a garnish of roasted sunflower seeds and a few *Lemon rings* (see page 135) or with a little amasake (see *Chestnut and amasake kuzu* recipe on page 145).

## Almond Butter

*110 g/4 oz almonds, 1 teaspoon umeboshi paste, grated rind of ½ lemon, 150 ml/¼ pt water, 1 tablespoon barley malt, rice syrup or maple syrup*

Wash and dry roast the almonds in a cast iron frying pan until they turn a light brown colour. Chop the almonds roughly and grind them to a powder in a coffee grinder. Mix the almonds in a suribachi or blender with the lemon rind, umeboshi paste and water and blend to a cream.

Place the cream in the frying pan and add the barley malt, rice syrup or maple syrup. The rice syrup gives a nicer colour to the cream than the barley malt. Heat the cream for 2 minutes, then whip it again briefly by hand and serve.

*Serving suggestions:* Almond butter is good on apple pies, *Baked pears with ginger sauce* (see below), *Hazelnut and ginger cookies* (see below), and *Couscous loaf* (see page 65).

## Hazelnut and Ginger Cookies

*170 g/6 oz rolled oats, 2 pinches sea salt, 6 tablespoons sunflower oil, 170 g/6 oz chopped hazelnuts, 1 tablespoon ginger juice (squeezed from freshly grated ginger), 60 g/2 oz grated carrot, 5 tablespoons barley malt*

Mix the rolled oats with the sea salt and rub in the sunflower oil. Mix in the chopped hazelnuts, ginger juice and grated carrot. Heat the barley malt in a saucepan until it becomes runny, then stir the oatflake mixture into the hot malt.

Oil a large bun tin and press the sticky cookie mixture firmly into the individual bun moulds with a fork. Bake at 180°C/350°F/Gas Mark 4 for 15 to 20 minutes until golden but not brown.

*Variations:* There are endless variations on this recipe. Try walnuts with lemon rind and juice or sunflower seeds, raisins and grated carrot.

*Serving suggestions:* These cookies could be served with *Amasake* (see page 144), *Almond butter* (see page 148), or *Dandelion coffee mousse* (see page 147).

## Baked Pear and Ginger Sauce

Serves 6.

*3 large conference or other sweet pears, 4 tablespoons barley malt, 1 tablespoon ginger juice (squeezed from freshly grated ginger)*

Wash the pears and cut them neatly in half. Scoop out the cores. Place each half face up on a baking tray and bake in a moderate oven for 10 minutes. Heat the malt and ginger juice in a saucepan for 2 minutes until the sauce is hot and runny, then pour it into the scooped out hole and over the pears. Bake for 5 more minutes then serve hot.

*Variations:* Make a barley malt and ginger sauce and crumble topping to go over the pears. Make the crumble mixture as in the *Apple and raisin crumble* recipe on page 144, and bake on an oiled baking tray in a moderate oven for 20 minutes. Make the sauce by bringing 425 ml/¾ pt water to a boil. Blend 2 tablespoons of kuzu in a little cold water, remove the pan from the heat and stir in the kuzu. Return to the heat and stir gently until the mixture thickens. Add 4 tablespoons of barley malt and 1½ tablespoons of ginger juice and simmer for 1 more minute. Pour over the halves of baked pear and sprinkle the crumble topping on top.

### Baked Apple with Raisins and Almonds

Serves 6.

*6 large eating apples, 140 g/5 oz raisins, 190 ml/⅓ pt apple juice, 1 tablespoon barley miso, 110 g/4 oz whole almonds*

Wash the apples and remove the cores to only three-quarters of the way through. Blend the miso with the apple juice and add the raisins. Simmer this mixture gently with a lid on until all the juice is absorbed into the raisins. Roast the almonds in a frying pan until they turn light brown, then chop finely. Mix the chopped nuts with the raisins and stuff this down the centre of the apples.

Preheat an oven to 180°C/350°F/Gas Mark 4 and place the apples in the centre of the oven for 10 to 15 minutes. Sometimes the apples split decoratively in the oven. It is pretty to score a ring around the apples ½ cm/¼ inch into the skin so that the apples split decoratively around the ring.

## Apricot and Cherry Pie

Serves 6.

*170 g/6 oz fresh cherries, 225 g/8 oz fresh apricots, 1½ tablespoons agar agar flakes, 570 ml/1 pt water, 1 tablespoon kuzu, 4 tablespoons rice syrup, 110 g/4 oz oatflakes, 225 g/8 oz strong white or wholewheat pastry flour, 6 tablespoons safflower oil, pinch of sea salt, water to mix*

Prepare the pie crust 1 hour in advance. Mix the oatflakes with the flour and salt. Stir in the oil with a spoon. Blend the water in slowly to make a stiff dough. Let the dough stand in a cool place for 30 minutes — in hot weather place it in the refrigerator. This makes a much better textured and less crumbly pastry.

Divide the dough in half and roll each half between 2 sheets of greaseproof paper until it is about 4 cm/⅛ inch thick. Put one piece of rolled pastry in a pie dish and bake blind for 10 minutes at 180°C/350°F/Gas Mark 4.

Wash and stone the fresh apricots and cherries. Cook the agar agar flakes in the water for 10 minutes then add the fruit and simmer for 10 minutes. Blend the kuzu with a little cold water, take the fruit off the heat and stir in the kuzu. Replace on the heat and stir until it thickens, then turn off. Mix in the rice syrup and allow to cool and gel slightly before placing in the prepared pie base.

Put the uncooked piece of pastry over the pie and flute the edges so that it sticks to the pie base. Cut 2 or 3 slits in the pastry top and bake at 180°C/350°F/Gas Mark 4 for 20 to 30 minutes until golden brown.

# 17.
# BEVERAGES

Here is a selection of healthy beverages. It is best to use a number of drinks at different times, as any one tends to become monotonous after a while.

## Three-Year Twig Tea (Bancha or Kukicha)

*½ tablespoon three-year twig tea per person, 290 ml/½ pt water per person*

Simmer the twigs in the water for 5 to 10 minutes, then pour through a tea strainer into your cup. Do not throw the twigs away, but simply add more of the twigs with more water to make your next brew. This can be continued for up to a week before throwing the old twigs away and starting afresh. It is very convenient to keep a certain saucepan or pot just for making this tea. A glass coffee jug that can be put onto a gas or electric stove is attractive and easy to use.

The first brew can be a little bitter, while later brews become more mellow and enjoyable. Experiment with the strength as some people enjoy it strong and others prefer it weak.

Three-year twig tea is also available in tea bags. Simply put the bag in a cup, pour boiling water over it, and let it sit for a few minutes before removing the bag. These are very useful to carry with you when you are out and about. Most cafes and restaurants are happy to give or sell you hot water to make your tea with. Better still, tell them where they can obtain these tea bags, so that they can provide them for you and their other customers. If you have any problems buying three-year twig tea bags, please look in the Appendix or page 160 for a list of suppliers.

*Serving suggestions:* An advantage of three-year twig tea is that it tastes pleasant without any milk or sugar. However if you are used to using these, you may like to add a little soya milk, barley malt, rice syrup or concentrated apple juice to it.

### Grain Coffee

There are now many varieties of grain coffee available in health and wholefood shops. Most brands are instant grain coffees, used in the same way as regular instant coffee. Some are quite delicious, others leave something to be desired. I prefer to use a natural grain coffee, that is simmered or percolated for 5 to 10 minutes in the same way as ground bean coffees. It is much more delicious and satisfying. One of the best types is Yannoh, made from a blend of 5 different grains and beans. If this is difficult to obtain, you can use the following recipe to make it yourself.

### Yannoh

*225 g/8 oz brown rice, 225 g/8 oz wheat, 110 g/4 oz aduki beans, 110 g/4 oz chick peas, 60 g/2 oz roasted chicory root*

Spread the rice and wheat out on one shallow baking tray and the aduki beans and chick peas on another. Roast in an oven at 180°C/350°F/Gas Mark 4 for 40 to 50 minutes until dark brown, but not black. Stir every 5 to 10 minutes so that the beans and grains roast evenly. The beans may need to be left slightly longer.

Mix the grains and beans with the roasted chicory root, then grind to a course powder in a coffee mill. Store in an air-tight jar. To make the coffee, simmer or percolate 1 tablespoon with 290 ml/½ pt water per cup for 5 to 10 minutes. Pour through a tea strainer into your cup.

### Dandelion Coffee

*½ tablespoon roasted dandelion root per person, 290 ml/½ pt water per person*

Be careful to pick a brand without any lactose or other additives. Simmer the roots in the water for 5 to 10 minutes, then pour through a tea strainer into your cup.

*Serving suggestions:* If dandelion coffee tastes a little bitter to you, add some barley malt or rice syrup. Malt goes particularly well with the taste of dandelion coffee.

### Sweet Kuzu Drink

*190 ml/⅓ pt water per person, 1 teaspoon kuzu per person, 1 to 2 tablespoons barley malt or rice syrup per person*

Bring the water to a boil, then take off the heat. Blend the kuzu in a little cold water and add to the pan. Put the pan back on a low heat and stir until the liquid thickens. Stir in the malt or syrup, then serve.

*Serving suggestions:* This is a good drink for children, who often love the sweetness and thick texture. *Hazelnut and ginger cookies* (see page 149) are nice dunked in a cup of sweet kuzu.

### Carrot Kuzu Drink

*190 ml/⅓ pt bottled pure carrot juice per person, 1 teaspoon kuzu per person*

Bring the carrot juice to a boil, then remove from the heat. Blend the kuzu in a little cold water and add to the pan. Replace on a low heat and stir for 2 to 3 minutes until the drink thickens.

*Serving suggestions:* Again this can be a popular drink with children, with its vivid colour and sweet taste.

### Umeboshi-Shoyu-Kuzu Drink

*290 ml/½ pt water per person, 1 teaspoon kuzu per person, 1 umeboshi plum per person, 1 teaspoon shoyu per person*

Blend the kuzu in 1 to 2 tablespoons of cold water. Bring the 290 ml/½ pt water to a simmer, add the kuzu and stir until it thickens. Add the umeboshi and shoyu, stir and break up the umeboshi. Pour into a cup and drink hot.

This special drink can be a very effective remedy for upset stomachs and intestines and can also be used as a 'pick-me-up' when feeling tired or devitalized.

# GLOSSARY

This glossary describes foods, methods of cooking, kitchen equipment and other terms that you may not be familiar with. You may need to refer to it often at first, but most of the words here should soon become familiar to you.

**Aduki beans**. Small, dark red beans, that may also be called adzuki or azuki beans.

**Agar agar**. White flakes or powder made from a sea vegetable. Used to make jellies and aspics.

**Amasake**. A sweetener made from brown rice or sweet rice and *koji* starter and allowed to ferment until sweet tasting.

**Arame**. A dark brown spaghetti-like sea vegetable. Usually cooked on its own or with vegetables as a main dish.

**Arrowroot**. A white starch powder made from the root of an American plant. Used to thicken sauces and desserts.

**Bancha tea**. See *Three-year twig tea.*

**Barley malt**. A thick, dark brown sweetener made from barley. Used to sweeten sauces, cakes, biscuits and other desserts.

**Black soya beans**. A black coloured bean of a longer shape than yellow soya beans.

**Bok choy**. A vegetable with large green leaves and thick white stems.

**Brown rice**. Rice that has only the tough outer husk removed, with the maximum amount of minerals, vitamins, fibre and protein. There are three main varieties, short, medium and long grain. Short grain is the most suitable for regular use in a temperate climate.

**Buckwheat**. A grain from a cereal plant native to Siberia. A very warming and strengthening grain, it is also used to make buckwheat noodles.

**Burdock**. A long, dark root vegetable that grows wild in Europe and America.

**Chinese cabbage**. A large, leafy vegetable rather like a cross between a cabbage and a crisp lettuce.

**Couscous**. A partially refined cracked wheat used in savoury and sweet dishes.

**Daikon**. A long, white radish, especially useful to serve with fish and deep-fried foods as it helps the digestion of fats and oils. Also called mooli.

**Dried daikon**. Dried and shredded *daikon* vegetable that is particularly good at dissolving fat deposits in the body.
**Dulse**. A reddish-purple sea vegetable mainly used in soups and salads.
**Fu.** A dried form of *seitan* made from wheat protein. It is available in thin sheets or thick round cakes.
**Ginger**. A yellow coloured root used in small amounts to add a hot, pungent taste to soups, stews, and other dishes.
**Gomasio**. A condiment to sprinkle on food, made from roasted sesame seeds and sea salt. It is also called gomashio and sesame salt.
**Grain coffee**. A coffee-like drink made from a variety of grains, beans and roots. It is caffeine-free and non-stimulating. Be sure to buy a variety without sugar or other additives.
**Green nori flakes**. Green flakes of a different variety of nori sea vegetable to that used to make sheets of nori. Used as a condiment and mild seasoning.
**Hiziki**. A dark brown or black spaghetti-like sea vegetable that is very mineral rich and has quite a strong taste. Usually cooked with vegetables as a main dish.
**Kelp**. A family of sea vegetables rich in minerals.
**Kinpira**. Sautéed carrot or carrot and *burdock* cut into matchsticks and seasoned with shoyu or tamari — a warming and vitalizing dish.
**Koji**. Rice inoculated with particular bacteria used to ferment rice or sweet rice in making *amasake.*
**Kombu**. A dark green sea vegetable with wide, thick fronds. It is mainly cooked with beans, as well as other vegetable dishes, to add to their digestibility, flavour and mineral content.
**Kukicha**. See *Three-year twig tea*
**Kuzu**. A white starch made from a long root growing in Japan and America. It is used for thickening sauces, vegetable dishes and desserts.
**Laver**. A sea vegetable similar to that used to make nori. It is sometimes boiled for several hours into a paste consistency and sold as laver bread.
**Macrobiotics**. An approach to natural and balanced living, based on applying yin and yang to diet, exercise, harmony with the environment and personal growth.
**Mekabu**. The base of the stems of the same sea vegetable used to make *wakame.*
**Millet**. A small, round yellow grain. It comes in many varieties.
**Mirin**. A cooking wine made from brown rice. It has a sweet taste.
**Miso**. A brown paste made from fermented soya beans, sea salt

and often a grain. Common varieties are barley miso (mugi miso), rice miso (genmai miso), hatcho miso and white miso. Barley miso is the best for regular use in seasoning soups and vegetable dishes. White miso is mainly used for seasoning sauces and dressings.

**Mochi**. Sweet rice pounded to a glutinous consistency. Used in savoury and sweet dishes, it can be made at home or bought ready-made in dried form.

**Mu Tea**. A tea made from a blend of either 9 or 16 non-stimulating herbs.

**Natto**. Soya beans that have been cooked, mixed with special micro-organisms, and fermented for 24 hours. It is rich in easily digested protein.

**Nishime**. A method of cooking vegetables with only a small amount of water to produce a full-flavoured and strengthening dish.

**Nori**. Thin black or dark purple sheets of a sea vegetable. Usually roasted over a flame until it turns green. Used to wrap around rice or noodles in making *sushi* and as a condiment and garnish.

**Organic foods**. Foods grown without the use of synthetic chemical fertilizers, herbicides, pesticides or fungicides.

**Rice syrup**. A thick, sweet-tasting golden syrup made from brown rice and barley. Used to sweeten drinks and many desserts.

**Rice vinegar**. A mild tasting vinegar made from brown rice or sweet rice, that is less acid-forming in the body than malt or cider vinegars.

**Sake**. Japanese rice wine, containing about 15 per cent alcohol.

**Seitan**. The protein extracted from wheat flour and cooked with kombu sea vegetable, shoyu and water. It can be made at home or bought ready-made.

**Shitake**. A dried mushroom with a strong flavour, traditionally used in Oriental cooking.

**Shiso**. Red, pickled leaves of the beefsteak plant, used to colour umeboshi plums and as a condiment.

**Shoyu**. A traditionally made soy sauce, made from soya beans, wheat and sea salt, fermented for over a year. It contains no sugar or chemical additives and is used frequently in place of salt to season vegetables, beans and other dishes.

**Soba**. Noodles made from buckwheat flour or a combination of buckwheat and wholewheat flour.

**Somen**. Very thin white or wholewheat Japanese noodles.

**Suribachi**. A mortar with fine serrations on the inside. It is supplied with a wooden pestle and used for grinding seeds, nuts, sea vegetables, sauces and dressings.

**Sushi**. Rice or noodles wrapped in *nori* sea vegetable, with fish or pickles in the centre and cut into rounds.
**Sushi Mat**. A fine bamboo mat used for making rolls of vegetables or grains, such as *sushi*.
**Sweet brown rice**. A rice that is sweeter and more glutinous than regular brown rice. Used in savoury and sweet dishes.
**Tahini**. A seed butter made from ground whole or hulled sesame seeds.
**Tamari**. A traditionally made soy sauce similar to shoyu.
**Tekka**. A condiment made by sautéing burdock, lotus root, carrot and root ginger with hatcho miso and sesame oil.
**Tempeh**. Cakes of soya beans bound together with a mould. Traditionally eaten in Indonesia and Sri Lanka, tempeh is high in easily digested protein. It is available in many good health or wholefood shops.
**Tempura**. A method of cooking vegetables, fish or seafood, by dipping in batter and deep frying.
**Three-year twig tea**. The twigs and leaves of mature tea bushes. Low in caffeine, it is an ideal tea to drink regularly.
**Tofu**. Soft, white cakes of soya bean curd. It is a protein-rich food, used in soups, vegetable dishes, dressings, spreads, and desserts.
**Udon**. Thin Japanese noodles made from wholewheat or wholewheat and unbleached white flour.
**Umeboshi**. Plums that have been pickled in sea salt and coloured with *shiso* leaves. They have a sour and salty taste, and are used as a seasoning. Also available in the form of a paste.
**Umeboshi vinegar**. A sour and salty tasting vinegar made from umeboshi plums.
**Wakame**. A sea vegetable coming in thin fronds, particularly suitable in soups.
**Wholefoods**. Foods as they come from nature, without chemicals and other additives or any parts being refined or taken away.
**Yang**. Energy or movement that is contracting. One of the pair of universal forces that create and sustain life and all phenomena.
**Yannoh**. A grain coffee often made from roasted rice, wheat, aduki beans, chick peas and chicory. It is percolated or boiled for 5 to 10 minutes as with regular bean coffee.
**Yin**. Energy or movement that is expanding. One of the pair of universal forces that create and sustain life and all phenomena.

# APPENDIX

FURTHER READING

## Cookery Books


Arasaki, Seibin and Teruko, *Vegetables from the Sea*, Tokyo, Japan Publications Inc., 1983.

Belleme, Jan and John, *Cooking with Japanese Foods*, Brookline, Mass., East West Health Books, 1976.

Bradford, Peter and Montse, *Cooking With Sea Vegetables*, Wellingborough, Thorsons Publishing Group, 1985.

Colbin, Annemarie, *The Book of Wholemeals*, New York, Ballatine Books, 1983.

Cowmeadow, Michele, *Macrobiotic Cooking*, Penzance, Cornish Connection, 1985.

Cowmeadow, Michele, *Macrobiotic Desserts*, Penzance, Cornish Connection, 1986.

Cowmeadow, Michele and Oliver, *Simple Feasts*, Penzance, Cornish Connection, 1987.

Esko, Wendy, *Introducing Macrobiotic Cooking*, Tokyo, Japan Publications Inc., 1978.

Jacobs, Barbara and Leonard, *Cooking with Seitan*, Tokyo, Japan Publications Inc., 1986.

Kushi, Aveline, *Aveline Kushi's Complete Guide to Macrobiotic Cooking*, New York, Warner Books, 1985.

Kushi, Aveline, *How To Cook With Miso*, Tokyo, Japan Publications, 1978.

Shurtleff, William and Akiko Aoyagi, *The Book of Miso*, New York, Ballantine Books, 1981.

Shurtleff, William and Akido Aoyagi, *The Book of Tempeh*, New York, Harper and Row, 1979.

Shurtleff, William and Akido Aoyagi, *The Book of Tofu*, New York, Ballantine Books, 1979.


## General Reading


Ballentine, Rudolph, *Diet and Nutrition*, Pennsylvania, The Himalayan International Institute Holesdale, 1978.

Cowmeadow, Oliver, *An Introduction To Macrobiotics*, Wellingborough, Thorsons Publishing Group, 1977.

Dufty, William, *Sugar Blues*, New York, Warner Books, 1975.

Kushi, Aveline, and Michio, *Macrobiotic Childcare and Family Health*, Tokyo, Japan Publications Inc., 1985.

Kushi, Aveline and Michio, *Macrobiotic Pregnancy and Care of the Newborn*, Tokyo, Japan Publications Inc., 1984.

Kushi, Michio, *Your Face Never Lies: An Introduction to Oriental Diagnosis*, Wayne, NJ; Avery Publishing Group Inc., 1983.

Kushi, Michio, with Alex Jack, *The Book of Macrobiotics*, Tokyo, Japan Publications Inc., 1987.

Kushi, Michio, with Alex Jack, *The Cancer Prevention Diet*, Wellingborough, Thorsons Publishing Group, 1984.

Kushi, Michio, with Alex Jack, *One Peaceful World*, New York, St.Martin's Press, 1987.
Kushi, Michio, with Alex Jack, *Diet for a Strong Heart*, New York, St.Martin's Press, 1985.
Miller, Saul, *Food For Thought: A New Look at Food and Behaviour*, NJ, Prentice-Hall Inc., 1985.
Sattilaro, Anthony, M.D., and Tom Monte, *Recalled By Life: The Story of My Recovery from Cancer*, Boston, Houghton-Mifflin, 1982.
Schauss, Alexander, *Diet, Crime and Delinquency*, Berkley, Parker House, 1981.

## EDUCATIONAL CENTRES AND DIETARY ADVICE

There are many teachers and educational centres offering classes on the theory of yin and yang and its practical application in cooking. The centres below can give you information on the nearest classes and help in your area.

**Great Britain and Europe**
The Community Health Foundation
188 Old Street
London EC1V 9BP, England
01-251 4076

**Canada**
Foundation Renouveau
4238 Rue Saint-Denis
Montreal, Canada
514-844 4153

**Australia**
Australian Macrobiotic Association
1 Carlton Street, Prahran
Melbourne 3181, Australia
03-529 1620

**USA**
East West Foundation
17 Station Street, Brookline
MA 02147, USA
617-738 0045

## MAIL ORDER FOOD SUPPLIERS

If you have any difficulties buying any of the foods used in this book, they can be obtained by mail order from the companies below. They also supply foods wholesale, so you may be able to get your local health or wholefood shop to buy them. You could also contact the educational centres given above for help finding your best local supplier of natural foods.

**Great Britain**
Clearspring Natural Grocer
196 Old Street
London EC1V 9BP
01-250 1708

**Canada**
Noah's Natural Foods Ltd
322 Bloor Street West
Toronto, Ontario M5S 1W5

**USA**
Mountain Ark Trading Company
120 South East Street
Fayetteville, AR 72701
501-442 7191